The Great Golden Garland of Gampopa's Sublime Considerations on the Supreme Path

Volume 2

A Modern, Liberal Version of Gampopa's Root Text
with Contemplative Contemporary Commentaries

by B. Simhananda

Printed and bound in Canada by Transcontinental, March 2011

©*The Great Golden Garland of Gampopa's Sublime Considerations on the Supreme Path — A Modern Liberal Version of Gampopa's Root Text with Contemplative Contemporary Commentaries.* Volume 2. B. Simhananda.

ISBN: 978-0-9809694-9-8

©2011 Orange Palm Publications

Registration of copyright: First trimester 2011
National Library of Quebec
National Library of Canada

Mailing address: Orange Palm Publications©
235 Rene Levesque Boulevard, Suite 310
Montreal, Quebec, H2X 1N8
Telephone: (514) 255-8700 ~ Facsimile: (514) 255-0478
E-mail: info@palmpublications.com
Website: http://www.palmpublications.com

Cover: Original Thangka painting, 'Gampopa' by Karma Tsering Lama
Illustations: Lucie Robitaille
Typesetting: Sareyu Honan Roy

All rights reserved. No part of this book may be reproduced in any form without permission in writing from the author except to quote, or photocopy, specific passages for the purposes of group study.

Other publications by the same author:

- *Jyoti for Kids — A Meditative Technique of Meditation by the Light*. Simhananda. 2010.
- *Towards a Transformative Photography*. Simhananda. 2010.
- *Scriptings of the Soul In Questions of Light — Simhananda's Little Book of Self-Inquiry, In 308 Contemplative Beads*. Simhananda. 2009.
- *Our Ordinary Extraordinary Earth and Its Extraordinary Ordinary People*. Simhananda. 2008.
- *Touch To This Earth Where Meanders Mankind*. Simhananda. 2008.
- *Buddhas, Bodhisattvas, Khadromas and the Way of the Pilgrim — A Transformative Book of Photography and Pithy Sayings*. Simhananda. 2007.
- *Holy-Moly Hiccoughs and Enigmatic Knotty Eructations From the Boffola Belly of Bu'Tai — The Drôleries and Dictums of Crazy Modern Dzog-zen*. Ken N.O. Sho. 2007.
- *Knots of Eternity — Paradoxes from Dadi to Daughter*. Volume 1. Dadi Darshan Dharma. 2007.
- *The Smiling Forehead — Paradoxes from Dadi to Daughter*. Volume 2. Dadi Darshan Dharma. 2007.
- *The Great Golden Garland of Gampopa's Sublime Considerations on the Supreme Path — Contemplative Contemporary Commentaries of Gampopa's Root Text*. Volume 1. B. Simhananda. 2005.
- *The Science of Full Moon Invocations — from Humanity's Heart to Hierarchy's Will; The Divine Concordance of Light III*. Dadi Darshan Dharma. 2007.
- *Seven Studies of Soul Stations or Soul-ar Progressions Upon Each of the Seven Cosmic-Physical Rays*; (an integral excerpt from Collectanea One, The Divine Concordance of Light). Etbonan Karta. 2007.
- *Seven Sacred Stations of the Self & Seven Flaming Fiats of Light Upon the Seven Cosmic-Physical Rays* (an integral excerpt from *The Divine Concordance of Light*). Etbonan Karta. 2001.
- *The Divine Concordance of Light: A Handbook from Heaven to Progression Earth—"The Seven Rays of God: Seven Studies of the Soul's Earthly Pilgrimage of Service Upon the Seven Cosmic-Physical Rays"*. Etbonan Karta. 2001.

Dedication

To the Venerable Gampopa,
the Incomparable Tsongkhapa and the
Inimitable Guru Rinpoche, Padmasambhava

"To these three great Incarnations,
I do humbly bow and prostrate myself."
May Buddha bless the bodhicitta intentions and
bodhisattva purposes of this most modest volume.

May the whole field of worldly merit
be thereby benefitted by it.

Table of Contents

Foreword 1 ix

Foreword 2 xv

Introduction 19

The Ninth Series of Ten Beads

A Modern, Liberal Version of Gampopa's Root Text
Mini Mala 9 23
Gampopa Beads 81 to 90
'The Ten Things upon which to Contemplate Mindfully, thereby Giving Rise
to the Ten Quickenings'

Simhananda's Contemporary Contemplative Commentaries on Gampopa's Root Text
Mahamudra Dzogchen Notes 9 35
Simhananda's Commentaries 101 to 110
The Ten Inspiriting Considerations Which Enhearten and Enhance the Path

The Tenth Series of Ten Beads

A Modern, Liberal Version of Gampopa's Root Text
Mini Mala 10 69
Gampopa Beads 91 to 100
The Ten Ways to Stray from Home Plate, Get Off Base, and Find Yourself Lost in Left Field

Simhananda's Contemporary Contemplative Commentaries on Gampopa's Root Text
Mahamudra Dzogchen Notes 10 81
Simhananda's Commentaries 111 to 120
The Ten Deviations or Desultory Wanderings to Avoid, Evade, or Shy Away From
whilst Peregrinating upon the Path

The Eleventh Series of Ten Beads

A Modern, Liberal Version of Gampopa's Root Text
Mini Mala 11 129
Gampopa Beads 101 to 110
The Ten Delusory Dilemmas of Man that ought to be Correctly Cognized and Astutely Apprehended, but can easily get Mind-Muddled and Mixed-Up, with their Jigsawed Antipodal Plight, or Genuine Counterpart

Simhananda's Contemporary Contemplative Commentaries on Gampopa's Root Text
Mahamudra Dzogchen Notes 11 141
Simhananda's Commentaries 121 to 130
The Ten Mix-Ups of Non-Identical Twins and Their Ensuing Embarrassments

Glossary 239

Foreword 1

Destiny, or karma, has made of me a Tibetan.

The love I feel for the people of Tibet whose lives over the past few decades have been suffused with suffering, waxes stronger with the passing of inexorable time.

In my bearing a greater amount of years than most of you, it stands to reason that I have borne witness to a greater passing panorama of horrific deeds than you may have experienced. Sometimes, the somber, dark side of man surfaces so strongly against life, that it stretches the confines of the spirit to still believe in his Divine nature.

In prevailing over all grim industry to destroy my people, the Tibetans have stood steadfast and survived all the multiple shocks and sufferings, physical as well as spiritual, bestowed upon them. Their transgressor and assailants have not succeeded to silence in them their intense spiritual flame, which even today, despite the atrocities endured, shines ever brighter.

Pilgrims ever fervent, and as sober and determined as they have been in the past, still come from all over the rugged confines and far-reaches of Tibet, and with holy feet and incessant chanting, prayer wheels and an inexhaustible number of prostrations, they still fill the roads and take to the high and winding by-paths that lead to the well-worn steps of their sacred monasteries.

The mantric sounds of 'OM AH HUM VAJRA GURU PADMA SIDDHI HUM' and 'OM MANI PADME HUM' are still heard subtly echoing within and without the hallowed walls of the Potola Palace, the Chenrezi-related residence which our spiritual head and leader, the Fourteenth Dalai Lama, was coercively forced to abandon.

Suffering has distressed my people for so long that they have nearly forgotten how to live without sorrow. Their multiple physical discomforts, their pauperism and privations, and their countless, ignominious humiliations have been transmuted and transformed by them into a more accelerated, heightened sacrificial initiation, due to their deep faith, religious ardor and strong spiritual maturity, all of which have been substantiated by centuries of time-honored, sacred teachings.

These sacred teachings have translated themselves into the estimable strength and indomitable spirit which make up the very fibre and well-being of the people of Tibet.

The Tibetan people must continue to quaff their spiritual thirst at the wisdom fount of these root teachings, since they are meant one wondrous day, as a united field of Divine consciousness to realize that state of Enlightenment which already, brightly pulses in their future Destiny's light.

It has always been part of the essence of wisdom to adapt and adjust all discourse, treatise and teachings to the particular time period, or era, wherein they are being transmitted. Did not the Buddha himself instruct and counsel the disciples of his own time period to 'not accept my teachings merely out of respect for me, but analyze and check them the way that a goldsmith would test the purity of a gold nugget, by rubbing it against a stone, hammering, or melting it'.

Buddhism, like man and mankind itself, must evolve and unfold to become an ever more refined, religious tool of interiorization and in consolidating it to an effective, external mode of expression, it must inspire the individuated consciousness to further awaken and become vigilant, heedful and more sensitive to the illusions of this world. Today's spiritual seeker who wishes to undertake the path of discipleship must follow a much more sinuous and difficult path than in the time epoch in which the venerable Master Gampopa lived.

Already, some nine hundred years have passed since Gampopa wrote a treatise that even today endures as an unerring guide for all those who desire to enjoin themselves to the pure-mindedness of the Buddha's Way, or the Buddhadharma.

This treatise which I myself have studied time and time again, encloses within its precious pages a numbered set and series of wise counsel and cautionary advice that serve as sublime indicators and superior pointers to the supreme path of service.

None can walk the path alone and unaided, and no-one today can consider himself immune to the nocuous effects of modern day living, so totally different in style and expression, than in Gampopa's day.

Nothing remains static, or inert. Buddhism must also reform, remold and remodel itself, while keeping close to its core essence. It must learn to adapt itself to the modern conscience and to the consciousness of the contemporary man, who desires to free himself from the bonds and bindings of his ignorance.

We do not live anymore in those past times where all transmitted instructions were accompanied by critical commentaries and clarified by an authentic, or competent instructor. Certain key teachings and practices today are not given out; or if they are, they tend to get out of hand, as they fall into the hands of authors, lecturers, and readers who inevitably fall victim to a biased, personal interpretation which I would, for the most part, qualify as unequivocally inadequate. Right reflection can only be skillful when the student stops mirroring his own navel vision and starts to seriously contemplate the wish-fulfilling jewels of his superior-seeing Mind.

The wisdom pearls written by Gampopa should be apprehended, discovered, and read through glasses untainted by the experiential ego. A correct reading polarizes self to Self and may contribute greatly to the soul's inward-forward progress.

This is exactly what B. Simhananda in his work and writings strives to accomplish. He masterfully steers and leads the reader through the labyrinthine twists and turns of his imperfections and frailties, to finally disembark him at his Being's terminal point of perfection. This present, partial adaptation of Gampopa's small spiritual opus cannot but help the disciple fight his ignorance on the battlefield of his own personality, where already, a sure victory refulgently shines.

This rendition of Gampopa's work, while solidly respecting the essence of his teachings, uses an original study approach which is more appropriate to the current condition of mankind and more attuned to his present evolution of mind. Solutions exist and they are uncovered, utilized and maximized in admirable and respectful fashion in this historic work, so skillfully adapted to the exigencies of the 21st century disciple.

I met B. Simhananda in Tibet at the time that he was writing this book. I supervised his work. On the whole it certainly was not an easy task for him, but the harvested results demonstrate to be more than satisfactory.

The author succeeds to render high homage to Gampopa and to honor with heart his precious teachings, whilst at the same time facilitating their integration into the modern human mind, mostly addicted to a steady diet of fast food, film and literature. Modern man desires too much, too fast, whereas what he really needs to do, is to take deep root within himself and take the time to learn how to learn, and to patiently integrate his ongoing spiritual apprenticeship.

I would at this point, before terminating this foreword, like to mention that the author of this opus has been my pupil and disciple for the duration of close to forty years. His life, obstacle-strewn as it has been, has not been an easy one. It has, however, helped in making, or fashioning out of him, a being who selflessly serves those High Beings 'of organized illumined minds', and of one who is devoted to loving mankind and who is entirely at the service of a hastily evolving humanity.

Although I have the dubitable reputation of being sparse in compliment, I must however, admit that this is a remarkable man and that his writings also cast a similar remarkable light. The rigorous discipline and training he has received under my supervision has made of him a most solid and reliable person. This book bears living testimony to his deep understanding and mastership of the Buddhist tenets and teachings.

In being my astute student, he has learned to discern the real from the false and to develop a superior sight in seeing beyond the mere appearance of the phenomenal world. I have hammered and rehammered the sworded metal of his pride, till today he wears only the honed empty scabbard of a true and sincere humility. His task is allied to mine and yoked are we, in our common desire to serve sentient humanity with intelligent compassion and evolutionary wisdom.

I would like to add that the beauty of a genuine teaching becomes apparent only after it has been punctiliously studied in its details and in the scrutiny of its directives. An authentic instruction must be thoroughly examined, put into practice and tested before it can reveal its veritable worth to the consciousness.

I would, therefore, highly suggest that the student study attentively the topics of thought contained herein, and that he methodically dissect the themes and commentaries written down in this book. Analyze them, manipulate them, practice them and test them out, and discover perhaps that it is not really the information, knowledges and wisdoms that you are testing, but throughout the whole paradoxical process, you are (unquestionably) putting yourself to trial.

Who am I wherefore, to make statements, declarations and suggestions as are found in this sober foreword?

I am but a simple Tibetan monk, the abbot of a monastery not very far distant from the area where Tsongkhapa took human birth.

On the physical plane, I have presently the charge, or responsibility, of supervising the spiritual development of approximately one thousand monks, somewhat scattered around the world. I travel but preciously little, preferring to remain with my people, and I choose for the greater part, to stay near, or within the peaceful confines of my monastery, with a numbered few of my devoted disciples. My true identity is of little importance, but to those who do know me, these few shall recognize me.

On this, the Buddha full moon celebration of the month of May, the year 2003, according to the western calendar,

I, with deep respect and universal Blessings, assign my initials as

> L.T.K., also known as the Tibetan

Foreword 2

Gampopa was a remarkable man and his writings were just as remarkable. In his ultimate wisdom, he knew intuitively how to transmit certain significant keys to our consciousness which would permit us to attain our own ultimate Realization... that is to say, our full Divine Potential which is situated way above what mere words can possibly convey.

The knowledge that wishes itself to be known at the conspicuous time of our first serious start upon the path of discipleship, reveals itself as necessary. Words take the guise of playing the role of being a fundamental support in the transmission of this particular knowledge which has to be known, studied, absorbed, and finally integrated into our Being... in order that the Divine Spark take birth, take root, and finally, irradiate forth Its own proper Knowledge.

This book will serve in the key capacity of being a precious guide to the disciple. The whole of it is transmitted in the occidental English language, and is adapted specifically to the occidental culture, but it is also, effectively and pragmatically, accessible to all those who peregrinate upon the arduous path of 'self transformation'. Difficult and exhausting is the Dharma Path but how truly 'full of grace' are its Teachings.

No one can be exempt from doubt, pain, or the suffering which is an inherent condition of this world. But each one of us can find rest and time-out for the reading of some sacred texts, and some time, also, to transmit upon our breath, whilst integrating some especially profound holy words, our deep love for the Divine, and the Divine's natural love for us.

To sensitively feel the SELF's EMPTY energy, and to hear Its silent percipient Hum upon our breath, is the Divine's primordial occult Link to our life, and this book will reveal to you the Secret Way to this Sacred Link.

Tibet abides within me, and the esoteric teachings that have been transmitted therein, (for centuries), flow integrally within my veins. In spite of the recurrent sufferings endured, and the repeated privations, sadness and misery that have been engendered by an unconscious humanity, I remain enduring and immutable in my Being.

The Essence of Tibet pulses and lives in me as it does, through all those who have inhabited this sacred land, who have taught there, and loved there. True Knowledge cannot be transmitted other than by the sacred ways of Authentic Love... Pure, Intangible and Intemporal.

I am what I am, and it is of little import what will happen to me. I know that I will continue to live through my writings, and in the hearts of all those who have contemplated, studied and put these into practice.

My Teaching is modern and oriented to the Occidental Mind, so that all may have access now, to this Occult Knowledge. My consciousness continues to evolve and so do my Teachings.

The Teachings adapt themselves as they ought to, and they transmit their energies according to the exigencies of the epoch. Only man hesitates, and refuses to change, through the irrational fear of his losing the precious gift of that specific energy formerly vehiculated, (or channeled), by the traditional, more ancient writings.

In order that modern man more deeply comprehend the contemporary, immemorial Teachings, then his own mode and particular modality of language must be used, so that he can have access to what is esoterically called, *real* knowledge. Speech then becomes a valuable gift, but words and speech without comprehension, count as nothing, if none of it can be used, to possibly *positively transform*.

There is a genuine need in using language, to utilize the Mental, or Mind vehicle, in order that a bridge, (or the Antakharana), be built between the small self and the High SELF.

Therefore, why doubt, or even hesitate, at a non-existent gate, before taking that definitive step that will inalterably lead the consciousness of man into the 21st century?

Sacred texts and truly sage words will always remain sacred and holy, and nothing can ever prevail enough to take away, or efface, the revelatory energy of the Truth, in man.

Nevertheless, to deliberately keep sacred texts and holy writings from adapting and modifying themselves to the exigencies of modern times, is equivalent to deliberately amputating their right to live, and it insentiently takes away their beneficent potential of transmitting the 'breath of Life' to all those whose consciousness, is actively thirsting for ever greater 'knowledge' and 'understanding'.

I have closely supervised this singular essay and render thanks to my esteemed disciple, Simhananda, for having accompanied me in this literary journey, where my beloved Tibet resonates so evocatively, within every thoughtfully written word, sentence, paragraph and page.

Tibet's energy circumambulates the reader and blesses him most profoundly. Its SPIRIT immerses, weaves and interweaves itself vibrationally through the innate wisdom found herein, in this volume. Tibet's vital energetic essence, circulates intimately and dynamically, within the SELF of whomever reads this book.

I shall be brief in saying that no one can remain insensitive to an in-depth reading of these pages.

To be able to fully open one's consciousness to the transcendental energy contained herein, is indisputably one of the finest gifts which can serve man, in his learning a great deal more about his inherent Divinity.

If Gampopa had lived in our present times, his precious teachings would echo forth with the same strength, deep wisdom and vigorous tonality, that are found to be occultly impregnating the sentences transmitted in this historic book, with perhaps the exception of two or three expressions remaining typically Tibetan.

Therefore, I bless unhesitatingly the precious Teachings which are contained within these pages.

To all those readers who would open and contemplate this book with a competent compassion, and in the conscious opening of their consciousness to the Higher SELF, I predict without any doubt whatsoever, that the sacred writings contained herein, will naturally flow toward their Nonself, (or ATMAN), as if they had issued from Lord Gampopa's personal pen.

May your High SELF rejoice, and Its Kingly Spirit peregrinate with you.

May you, the reader, take a significant step toward the divine radiancy of your full Buddha Potential.

Master L.T.K.,
The TIBETAN
March 11, 2011

Introduction

Gampopa was indeed a Dharma Lord. He knew the intricacies of the Way, just as Tsongkhapa clearly and progressively envisioned It, and Milarepa sang his poetic laudations of It, and that Marpa, Naropa and Tilopa before him, and down through Atisha, (and the whole Kadampa lineage), the Mahasiddhas, the Arhats, and the Buddha Himself, KNEW.

The perfect and powerful oral instructions of Milarepa, taken down and condensed by Lord Gampopa's disciplined, terse, and impeccable penmanship, have given to the world a superb, almost supreme, step-by-step guide book to the peak of progressive enlightenment.

Spike by spike, his pen-strokes strike accurately and succinctly, the key acu-nâdî nerve-points of inner Mount Meru, which ineluctably leads the spiritual climber, progressively up to the heights of spiritual wisdom.

How many monks, students and disciples over the last nine centuries, (I wonder), have succeeded to plant their flag of (ultimate) freedom under the clear skies of an illumined consciousness, due to this clear-headed Lama Lord's instructions, and to his obvious, deep compassion for the struggling seeker of enlightenment?

In appreciation for the numerous (past) times the author of this present treatise has himself studied and benefitted greatly, (over a series of Tibetan incarnations), from Gampopa's pithy, synthetic shastras on the sutras of Essence Mahamudra, he has set for himself the humble task of rendering and commenting upon these in the modern English idiom, and in today's contemporary style of written expression.

To this end, he hopes to have accomplished this in such a way that the present generation of students and readers of Buddhist literature and philosophy, will appreciate 'Gampopa's Precious Garland' in a new mode of understanding, so that all who may peruse, or assiduously study this work, will be greatly benefitted.

Gampopa's partial treatise put forth herein, is to be divided into a tripartite set of ten advisory points each, called Mini Mala, or Garland Beads.

Each set of ten beads encapsulates a modern liberal rendition, or contemporary, free translation, (sometimes expanded), of Gampopa's Root Text... which at the beginning of each of the three principal chapters is written, compiled, and sectionized under the canopied appellation of Mini Mala IX, X, and XI. Interestingly enough, each subject matter and its thematic phrasing, (within the chapter), moves forward pertinently, as would a progressive series of prayer beads upon an imagined, or mentalized mala.

But, in complete alignment with Tibetan tradition, the greater bulk or preponderance of critical thought, creatively elucidated and graphically delineated in each extended chapter, remain the author's, (B. Simhananda's), own 'Contemplative Contemporary Commentaries', (C.C.C.), on Gampopa's Root Text.

The present author has inventively organized these 'Contemplative Contemporary Commentaries', under the umbrella appellation of "Mahamudra Dzogchen Notes" 9, 10, 11, which in this premier book opens with the Ninth Mini Mala, originally dealt with by Gampopa.

Notwithstanding, it would be advantageous for the reader to observe that the Simhananda commentaries, (C.C.C.'s), do not necessarily follow 'Gampopa's Golden Garland' to the bead... even though they are generally and collectively classified by a central theme, corresponding to the original root text.

Nor does the cumulative number of B. Simhananda commentaries, (C.C.C.'s), in the book, necessarily follow to the tee the actual set number, sequence and discursive disquisition, of the great Lord Gampopa's thematic thoughts from the root text.

The reader will sometimes be called upon to relate the two corresponding texts, that is, Gampopa's and Simhananda's, rather intuitively, instead of logically.

Cognitive contemplation and insight meditation on the varied topics of correlated thought is highly suggested for the correct grasp, or synthetic comprehension, of both styles of presentation. The student must go at it slowly, progressively and steadily in disciplined study, before the flower of intuitive mentation can possibly bloom forth, in blessings of subtle understanding.

Humble hearing from humble reading will keep the spirit of 'Gampopa's Precious Garland' alive, in this fresh rendition of this ultimately classic work of Buddhist philosophical thought.

May the Buddhadharma live on, and may Lord Gampopa's spirit continue to be honored in every serious practitioner's heart.

In submitting the sincere 'souhait' that all sentient beings benefit beneficently from this modest treatise, the present author, B. Simhananda, extends his goodwill to one and all with whatever blessings that the Buddha, in his Infinite Wisdom, may have generously bestowed through his pen.

In closure, the author proffers a deep, heartfelt gratitude for the kind words of his own Lama Lord, which are to be found in the simple, but profoundly touching Forewords, to this labor of love.

B. Simhananda
Montreal, May 8, 2003
Re-edited March 11, 2011

Mini Mala IX

The NINTH SERIES of Ten Beads from
Gampopa's Golden Garland

Gampopa Beads 81 to 90

The Ten Things upon which to Contemplate Mindfully, thereby Giving Rise to the Ten Quickenings

Gampopa's Root Text
Bead 81

Contemplating upon the rare multivaried richness which is this life and upon the individual gemlike preciousness of this body, quicken yourself to accommodate, arrogate and advocate the divine Dharma.

The Ten Things upon which to Contemplate Mindfully, thereby Giving Rise to the Ten Quickenings

Bead 82

Contemplating upon the inescapable ordeal which is the onslaught of the death experience, quicken yourself to cultivate a proper moral excellence; and bend your mind and will to the refinement of spiritual practice, and its cultivated discipline.

Bead 83

Contemplating upon the automatic, often negative consequences which attend the Law of Karma, quicken yourself to abdicate all dharmic delinquency, and get yourself definitely out of the chaos of nocuous iniquity.

The Ten Things upon which to Contemplate Mindfully, thereby Giving Rise to the Ten Quickenings

Bead 84

Contemplating upon the mean man's slavery to karmic cycles and of his being's thralled serfdom to samsara, quicken yourself to realize a true Liberation and to effectuate a full Freedom, in this very lifetime.

Bead 85

Contemplating upon the suffering, pain and pathos of people ensnared in samsara, quicken yourself to a bold and enheartened enkindling of compassionate bodhichitta.

The Ten Things upon which to Contemplate Mindfully, thereby Giving Rise to the Ten Quickenings

Bead 86

Contemplating upon the generalized mental confusion of people everywhere and their abject lack of clarity, quicken yourself to quietly ponder everything and learn to meditate actively... so that the mind can stand independently clear of all disquiet, and therewith emptied, rest in deep inner peace.

Bead 87

Contemplating upon the fact that confusion and delusion are both bad habits of the mind, and are difficult addictions of the psyche to extirpate, quicken yourself to an increased exhortation of meditational practice, and of restorative but sharp sadhana.

The Ten Things upon which to Contemplate Mindfully, thereby Giving Rise to the Ten Quickenings

Bead 88

Contemplating upon the mad frenzy, fast fury and fierce force of the five afflictive 'kleshas' besetting man in this crippling Kali age, quicken yourself to apply with promptitude, the proper preventive (attitudinal) prophylactic; or the appropriate, antipodal (affective) cure, to all debilitating poisons that are associated with the contra-positive passions.

Bead 89

Contemplating upon the troubled times of this defiled and demoralizing age of decay and decline, quicken yourself to meet the challenge of adversity with extra doses of patience, composure and containment, well-peppered with dispassion.

The Ten Things upon which to Contemplate Mindfully, thereby Giving Rise to the Ten Quickenings

Bead 90

Contemplating upon how life sails by in the wink of an eye, and how one can willy-nilly be spun around silly and dizzy with untold number of senseless, superficial distractions, (until one's life is totally spent into a heaping stockpile of absurd insignificance), quicken yourself to use spiritual Intent with industriousness, earnestness, and unremitting high purpose.

These then are the constituted end of the listed **"Ten Things upon which to Contemplate Mindfully, thereby Giving Rise to the Ten Quickenings"**.

Mahamudra-Dzogchen Notes 9

SIMHANANDA's
Contemporary Contemplative Commentaries on the
NINTH SET of Ten Beads of Gampopa's Root Text

Thematically entitled: **The Ten Inspiriting Considerations Which Enhearten and Enhance the Path**

Simhananda Commentaries 101-110
(In correlation with Gampopa's Mini Mala 9, Beads 81-90)

Simhananda's Contemporary Contemplative Commentary
101

Our life is the gift of Existence itself to that part of us which is human.

Our body is the gift of human incarnation to that part of us which is Divine.

Existence, somewhere along the line of Timelessness, gave us a beginning, (a first birth), within the beginningless frame of a wonderful world... spontaneously arising and manifestly appearing as a mysterious process of constant creativity, within a show of infinitely varied, apparent phenomena.

To have been given such a rare opportunity to live within such a world of seemingly constrictive, (albeit progressive), evolutionary development... and through the resources of the enlightened means of Dharma study and practice... to have the opportunity to study, know and transcend the ordinary mind, and to realize the mind's relative duality as being fully coemergent with that of absolute nonduality... is indeed an uncommon challenge, a remarkable calling, and an extraordinary spiritual undertaking.

C. C. C. 101-2

The ongoing human condition of duality, of present pain and pleasure, and the evolutionary process of meriting Initiation, proffers to man the extremely experimental and auspicious adventure of introducing, bringing down, and divinely implanting upon planet earth, the Adamantine Mind and Resplendent Form of the Primal Buddha of Activity.

It goes without saying that our coming to earth, that is, the act of taking birth, is derived from an a priori collection of Merit which comes arcanely from elsewhere, and is occultly downloaded along with us to this present earth endeavor... where a new collection of Merit is to be re-actively undertaken... proper to the bodhisattva services rendered, for the happiness and sake of all sentient beings, everywhere, and in the interest of all interconnected, interlocked and interdimensional sentiency, wherever found.

C. C. C. 101-3

Being here-now temporarily earth-bound, we strive and suffer upon the positively and negatively, polarized mind-streams of contracting and expanding consciousness; and undertake the subjective quest of generating a reforming, transcentral 'collection of golden wisdom', by means of our personally becoming via the Dharma, a conquering Buddha of Enlightened Awareness.

Therefore, we should understand the great import and imperative of the daily recitation, or restating, of our Bodhisattva vow, for the future-now Maitreya Buddha is already on His way down from Tushita Heaven... and is ready to take His promised place, (beside us), within our future-present and purified Bodhicitta form.

Hence, with this aforementioned knowledge set firmly in mind, it is our responsibility to go forth into the world and clearly sound the correct note of the Dharma.

It is up to us to present and demonstrate to receptive souls everywhere, all of the gradual and appropriate spiritual practices, for the greater keepsake and glory of all sentient beings, on earth, as in heaven.

The Ten Inspiriting Considerations Which Enhearten and Enhance the Path

C. C. C. 102

Life is impermanent, death is sure.
Life is transient, death is sure.
Life is short, death is sure.

Life is insubstantial, you are mortal.
Life is nondurable, you are mortal.
Life is frail, you are mortal.

Life is flying by, death is coming.
Life is passing by, death is coming.
Life is comet-like, death is coming.

Life is a fly-by-night experience.
Death flies by anytime, (anywhere).

So, my frail one, flit not your life away;
for precious and pure, and rare a gift,
it surely is.

Practice probity, show right conduct, gather merit, (to positively affect your next life), and be disciplined in divagating the Dharma path... for death is nearer to you now, than yesterday.

C. C. C. 103

'What goes round today comes round tomorrow', so the saying goes.

'Harm another today and hurt yourself tomorrow.'

'Get downright angry today and you get total angst tomorrow.'

'Pepper negatively the soup of today and your stomach burns the whole darn day tomorrow.'

In short, (and please excuse the crudeness): 'Shit on today and tomorrow stinks!'

However, from a positive perspective, consider the following thoughts:

'Take good care of today and tomorrow will take good care of you.'

'Be happy today and tomorrow will smile upon you, in return.'

'Be undisturbed today, and tomorrow won't dare disturb you, even if someone does his best, (to upset you).'

'Serve selflessly all sentient beings today, and tomorrow, who knows, the Buddha Himself may serve you.'

C. C. C. 103-2

In other words: 'Do positive deeds today and tomorrow's negative karma timidly absconds.'

In resume: 'Practice dharma impeccably today and samsara will definitely quit the scene sometime, (someday), tomorrow.'

C. C. C. 104

Samsara is suffused with suffering of the most subtle of sorts, such as mere (apparent) existence and the mere process of dualistic thinking... to the more obviously gross of sorts, such as (apparent) sickness, pain, emotional hurt, agitation, ignorance and death.

Human birth is, (so far), a process of (evolutive) suffering.

Craving, or grasping at anything, even beauty, is suffering.

Separation is suffering. Work, struggle, strife, even exercise is suffering.

Writing, composing and all the creative arts is suffering.

Prayer and penance, and yes, even practice, (that is, sadhana, or spiritual discipline), is suffering.

Standing up and sitting down, (upholding a good posture), is suffering.

All movement, (going pro, or against the nature of friction, resistance and gravity, e.g. walking, swimming, yoga, or running), even when done with exhilaration, is a (subtle) suffering.

Bracing the cold and soaking in the heat is suffering.

The Ten Inspiriting Considerations Which Enhearten and Enhance the Path

C. C. C. 104-2

Getting up in the morning and facing the mirror is suffering.

Honest communication and right understanding is suffering; aspiration and yearning is suffering.

Bearing and balancing the horizontal and vertical crosses of life is suffering.

The sensibility of the senses and the sensitivity of sensing, is suffering.

Breathing-in-and-out is suffering; sitting in zazen is suffering; studying is sure suffering.

Beholding a rose is (aesthetic) suffering; and undergoing bliss is blissful suffering.

When and where pain meets pleasure and pleasure pain, is suffering.

Copulating is suffering; the face (and cry) of orgasm is suffering; the mask of no orgasm is suffering.

Eating, digesting, burping and shitting is suffering.

C. C. C. 104-3

Putting on one's socks and pulling them up is suffering; putting on one's sandals and taking a first step is suffering.

Starting the day, (on the right foot), is suffering.

Opening one's heart is suffering; opening one's legs is suffering.

Sex, (or no sex), is suffering, (but it disguises itself as pleasure, or sublimation).

Being a saint is ecstatic suffering; so is the masochist's gratification.

Being selectively unhappy is suffering; being cruel, (or willfully evil), is suffering.

Daily life is diurnal suffering; just being alive is (existential) suffering.

Ergo, it stands to reason that the motivation to be liberated from all samsaric existence, and therefore, from suffering, is a good and worthy goal.

C. C. C. 105

Samsara strongly suggests that the wheel of the world whirls around in a whirl of woe, whimper and wound.

Awaken and get a whiff of the suffering.

Let yourself be profoundly stirred and empathize deeply with the sad, sad song of universal suffering that is being chanted throughout life by all sentient beings.

And let yourself be moved to generating an even greater bodhicitta and infinite compassion for all of these suffering ones of the Buddha's devoted children, everywhere.

Consciously determine (now) to do continual puja for the suffering, on the altar of your Awakening Heart.

C. C. C. 106

Consider that within the worlds of samsara, wrong view is the norm.

The very fact of automatically thinking that the apparent, phenomenal world is reality, causes duality and dual thought to bind and bend the ordinary mind into delusion; and consequently, in such a way, mental distortion becomes a major source of suffering amongst the unawakened.

Therefore, as an astute student of the Dharma law and of its principal tenets, it is your serious responsibility to listen attentively, reflect deeply and analyze insightfully, (the Master's talks). You must be conscientiously absorbed in some form of post-contemplative tranquility.

Finally, without fail, you, as the dedicated disciple, must learn to discriminate sharply, before integrating any important knowledge into your (own) book of Wisdom.

C. C. C. 107

It may be a shocking surprise to hear that basic ignorance is probably our worst habit of mind. Ignorance is faulty perception at its worst. It is something so insidiously subtle that we make, (or recreate), this mistaken notion, (this flawed view), over and over again. So long as we remain ignorant, we shall continue to do so ad infinitum, far into the future... as we have always done so, in the past, as far back even, as beginningless time.

Basic ignorance has no end, no beginning. Somehow, naturally or artificially, it just is, (or seems to be), not only as an earthly condition, but universally so, as if the very stuff of creation was stuffed with it.

However, like most dilemmic paradigms, there is an apparent way out of the whole delusional shebang.

The sheer emptiness of the Big Lie is readily available to whomsoever faces the sheer emptiness of the Void, and is genuinely ready for Liberation.

C. C. C. 107-2

It is impossible to trace ignorance back to its illusional, (non-substantial) roots; nor to its delusional effects, as a rational resultant.

It is a blatant waste of time and dissipated effort.

Note, however, that upon true Liberation the student finds himself in a snap, freed from the whole empoisoning process of ignorance, and the whole imprisoning play of maya.

The Holy Dharma is the sacred door to that Way out.

Therefore, as dedicated students, be exhorted, as well as inspired, to study, practice and train in the ways and byways of the Holy Dharma, day in and day out... in order to reach enlightenment and its concomitant, Ultimate Liberation.

C. C. C. 108

If the mind is disturbed, the emotions will usually follow suit.

Conversely, if the emotions are shifted, shafted, or shocked into afflictive upset, then the mind, in following the brunt of the aftershocks crashing into it, will usually, (most of the time), follow suit and be thrown off balance.

What follows is, ergo, a relatively copious list of some fifty examples, illustrating how the mind may affect, (or infect), the emotional body and how conversely, if you reverse them, the emotional body can adversely affect, or pollute the mind.

This is perhaps the reason why bipolarized, or dualistic thought, is often referred to as being affected, swayed, influenced, or interested thought, as it is most always highly impressed, (and sometimes, even impaired), by the aura, intent and color of the emotional body.

The whole subconscious process is conditioned as well, by other subtle factors which involve the intricate imposition of the law of duality upon the ordinary (robotic) mind, with its discernible resultant, being that of (deceptive) delusion.

C. C. C. 108-2

Here then, is a cogent rudimentary list made for the astute mind of the serious sadhaka, and to which list there can always be added a still greater enumeration, creating a more personal and discerning, accurate cataloguing.

Since, in the immediately following passages, we are critically capitalizing upon those degenerate and disturbing emotions which are found to be especially rampant in the present Kali period, or dark age, and which pointedly affect the mind, darkly, negatively, or involutively... the ensuing exemplary list will hold true to this peculiarly biased theme and not place, (for the moment), any uncalled-for attention upon the more positively polarized states, or influences, of mind and emotion.

Fifty Examples of
the False Mind, Negatively Affecting the Emotions

1. The mind which is agitated enlists the restless emotions.

2. The mind which is distracted enlists the sensually-incited emotions.

3. The mind which is unsettled enlists the disquieting emotions.

4. The mind which is disturbed enlists the perturbing emotions.

5. The mind which is defiled arouses the impure emotions.

6. The mind which is uncharitable arouses the unloving emotions.

7. The mind which is doubtful arouses the uneasy and perplexed emotions.

8. The mind which is arrogant arouses the peacock-like and prideful emotions.

C. C. C. 108-4

9. The mind which is greedy provokes the grasping emotions.

10. The mind which is angry provokes the hurtful emotions.

11. The mind which is lustful provokes the covetous emotions.

12. The mind which is desirous provokes the needy emotions.

13. The mind which is self-centered engages the narcissistic emotions.

14. The mind which is prejudiced engages the preferential emotions.

15. The mind which is self-willed engages the selfish emotions.

16. The mind which is undisciplined engages the self-indulgent emotions.

C. C. C. 108-5

17. The mind which is indignant stirs up the wrangling emotions.

18. The mind which is aggressive stirs up the warring emotions.

19. The mind which is infuriated stirs up the (very harmful), killing emotions.

20. The mind which is argumentative stirs up the contentious, clashing emotions.

21. The mind which is discouraged induces the disheartened emotions.

22. The mind which is despondent induces the depressed emotions.

23. The mind which is despairing induces the desperate emotions.

24. The mind which is defeated induces the discomfited emotions.

C. C. C. 108-6

25. The mind which is unhappy inveigles the heartsick emotions.

26. The mind which is miserable inveigles the miserly emotions.

27. The mind which is sorrowful inveigles the sad emotions.

28. The mind which is grieving inveigles the tearful emotions.

29. The mind which is unforgiving fetches the unpardonable emotions.

30. The mind which is resentful fetches the bitter emotions.

31. The mind which is envious fetches the jealous emotions.

32. The mind which is cynical fetches the acrimonious emotions.

33. The mind which is morose bestirs the moody emotions.

34. The mind which is gloomy bestirs the dark emotions.

35. The mind which is sarcastic bestirs the sour emotions.

36. The mind which is humorless bestirs the short-tempered, (ill humored), emotions.

C. C. C. 108-7

37. The mind which is frightened jogs to attention the fearful, faltering emotions.

38. The mind which is neurotic jogs to attention the afflictive emotions.

39. The mind which is worried jogs to attention the fretful emotions.

40. The mind which is terrified jogs to attention the dread, (direful) emotions.

41. The mind which is muddled foments the mixed-up, confused emotions.

42. The mind which is burdened foments the heavy, oppressive emotions.

43. The mind which is hysterical foments the crazed, seething emotions.

44. The mind which is possessed foments the wild-eyed, raving-mad emotions.

C. C. C. 108-8

45. The mind which is (highly) critical enflames the judgmental, condemnatory emotions.

46. The mind which is hypocritical enflames the guileful, two-faced, smooth-spoken, feigning of (true) emotions.

47. The mind which is mendacious enflames the falsely-colored, false-hearted, faithless emotions.

48. The mind which is treacherous enflames the deceitful, unfaithful, perfidious, Judas-kissed emotions.

49. The mind which is unenlightened, underwrites the whole array of (erroneous), negative emotions.

50. The mind which is uncompassionate, patronizes all of the self-seeking, self-interested, self-centered, self-remembering, Self-neglectful, other-forgetting, churlish emotions.

C. C. C. 108-9

And so ends the moderately long list of fifty negatively-polarized examples of mind influencing emotion, (and conversely), of emotion affecting mind.

May it be suggested, as a beneficial mind exercise, and for the building of character, that the student study and practise the application of the 'antidote' to this negatively-polarized sample of examples, and set about to dynamically re-create the list, in definitely more positive terms.

C. C. C. 109

Bodhicitta should inspirit and nurture your resolve to polish the paramita of patience.

Modern times, despite the technological conveniences which serve to ease our lives and augment our comfort, are not necessarily, easy times.

The decibel noise level alone which is rampant in the world, is enough to drive any serious meditator to an almost dhyanic despair.

The atmosphere is filled with T.V., radio, video, Nintendo, Play Station, I-Phones, D.S.'s, DVDs, and CDs; not to mention all of the sub-auditory signals like sonar, microwave, lazer and specialized computer electronics, space stations, LFW weapons and many other secret conspiracies of questionable (sinister) intention... all vying in a non-declared, non-official war, for the singular attention and ultimate control of the mind.

The Ten Inspiriting Considerations Which Enhearten and Enhance the Path

C. C. C. 109-2

And then, of course, we have every country's indispensable transportation department — another requisite junta of aggressiveness, (via pandemic noise), directed against the elevation of consciousness.

And in this sphere of operations, we point out but a few foul culprits, or obvious guilties... such as automobiles, buses, trucks and vans; racecars, motor-boats, race boats, cruise boats, atomic and nuclear submarines; motored rickshaws, subways, trains, aeroplanes and helicopters; motorcycles, snowmobiles, 3-wheelers, 4-wheelers; hockey, baseball, football and soccer matches, roller skate derbies and freestyle skateboarding competitions.

Next, we have the very vocal, human voice pollution — for example, loud speech, (loudspeakers), yelling, screaming, angry talk, university debate teams, parliamentary disputes, arguments of all kinds, verbal diarrhea, verbal aggression, verbal barrages (e.g. in wrestling), verbal violence and abuse (in homes and the workplace); loud, bad mouthing, show-off musical voices, screeching songs, vociferous DJs, boisterous sportscasters, matter-of-fact, somber newscasters, repetitious T.V. commercials, bland, boring weathermen, swaggering evangelists, popular hosts and special guest shows, and calls to public prayer, healings, and donations.

C. C. C. 109-3

Not to mention, of course, all the aberrant, negatively charged, discursive thoughts that are perpetually and inaudibly projected outwards into the environment; and the constant monkey chatter, and chicken clucking, and maddening cognitive roar that passes for intelligent inner dialogue within the common, subjective mind.

Ah, what to do, what to do?

There are a lot of unconscious people out there, a lot of insensitive human beings, a lot of bums, beggars and buggers whose main task is to keep any bodhisattva-vow practitioner away from the contemplative mind, but rather, in the full practice of patience, patience and patience... and this, without complaint for the remainder of a longsuffering lifetime... spent in the conscious, difficult accumulation of (golden) merit.

Ah, what karmic opportunity!

C. C. C. 110

Life is important!

The dynamics of Life's evolutionary process comes always charged with the golden opportunity to positively generate enough bodhicitta to attain first, enlightenment, and perhaps, thereafter, Liberation.

However, a Buddhist precondition to Liberation, (via Realization), has always been the innate clause that all attained Freedom should be used for the kindly benefit and greater benefaction of all beings.

Therefore, be ever diligent and vigilant when peregrinating the path of Dharma.

Do not merely drag yourself along (the Way); don't you dare be a drag, and drag (the) Dharma down.

Discipline is absolutely indispensable. Training is always imperative. Practice is (utterly) precious.

C. C. C. 110-2

Through rational analysis and contemplative insight, you will see for yourself, (and realize), the utmost importance of an eager engagement and steady diligence... both of which are essential in the specialized field of spiritual sadhana and gradual Self awakening. The Bodhisattva goal of uncompromising service towards all, is to be secured in this one lifetime.

Therefore, take heart, because with an engaged enthusiasm upholding you and with the means of skillful effort, the day will soon dawn when all discipline, training, and practice will become (for you), an exercise and training activity filled with the simplicity and joy of a (natural) effortlessness. In other words, a true delight.

C. C. C. 110-3

You will, in short order, be well on your way and ready to pursue and tackle the higher aspects of mind, virtue and wisdom — and no more, will you suffer the weary feeling that you are 'sacrificing'.

But every significant step of the way toward eventual Buddhahood, (come what may), will spring with a spontaneous joy, and will thus become a broad source of continued happiness, and you will, therewith, be filled with a deep peace.

Therefore, students, sadhakas and disciples, do what you must and do what you have to do, in holding nothing back on the path of Dharma.

Let laziness do its lazy stuff, and loll around in somebody else's backyard hammock.

C. C. C. 110-4

Let go of all trivial, or insignificant activities, that seem to bring out external reward and (so-called) respect, self-importance, ephemeral fame, or a sense of (proud, puffed-up) achievement; or a sense of hung-up on oneself thrills and excitement; or any sort of self-esteem derived from a seeming appearance of constant busyness... and all hustle, bustle, fuss and flurry of activity which is but presumptuous, often pompous stuff, that is, bottom line be said, essentially 'meaningless'.

As seen in the clear light of day with a clear mentality, (when you at last wake up), the all of it is of short-lived and of little benefit, and certainly, of no lasting advantage to anyone, especially to your Self.

An unimportant bit of advice: 'Go up the evolutionary ladder, not down the involutionary snake'.

C. C. C. 110-5

It goes without saying that the correct understanding of all authentic Buddhist philosophy and literature, with their innumerable meanings and subtleties of interpretation, and their complex permutations of cognitive and contemplative thought, is not an easy undertaking — it's hefty stuff.

But if the sadhaka tackles it slowly a step at a time, a shastra, or a sutra at a time, a spiritual state or developmental stage at a time, day-in and day-out, under the kind and loving guidance of a Lama Lord, or teaching Rinpoche, then clear understanding will ineludibly dawn, (one cloudless day), along with the clear light of humble Achievement.

Do not get discouraged.

Take your time, and create the personal space within your psyche, wherein your inherent vim, vigor and vigilance will be naturally disposed to actively rise, and determine to accept warmheartedly the challenge of (potential) Buddhahood.

C. C. C. 110-6

Have confidence in the Holy Dharma, and you will see that 'enlightened endurance' will come, and that it will serve with a will of its own, your Bodhisattva Vow.

Spiritual staying power will then be yours for all time, whenever called upon.

Do your best, your real best, and be Blessed.

These then, are Simhananda's contemporary, contemplative commentaries regarding **"The Ten Inspiriting Considerations Which Enhearten and Enhance the Path"**.

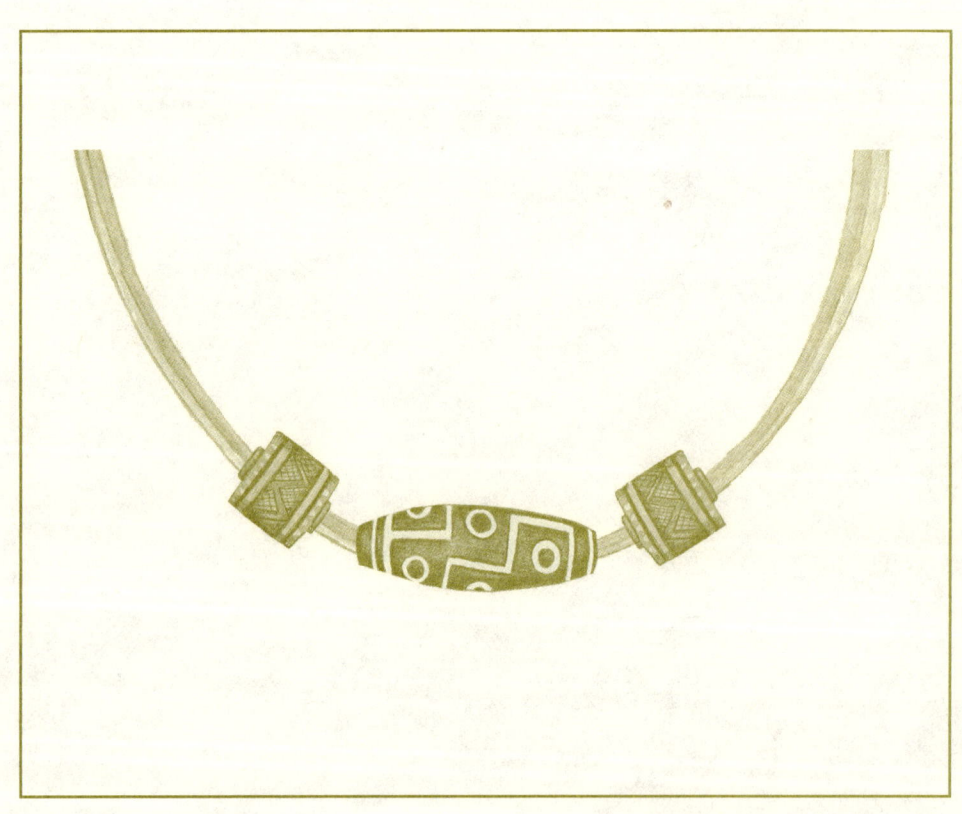

Mini Mala X

The TENTH SERIES of Ten Beads from
Gampopa's Golden Garland

Gampopa Beads 91 to 100
**The Ten Ways to Stray from Home Plate,
Get Off Base and Find Yourself Lost in Left Field**

Gampopa's Root Text
Bead 91

If at home plate you have little faith but your base knowledge is far and wide, you may just find yourself lost in the left field of gallivanting platitudes and galling garrulousness.

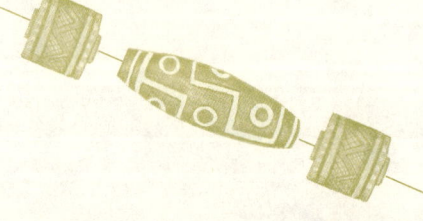

The Ten Ways to Stray from Home Plate, Get Off Base and Find Yourself Lost in Left Field

Bead 92

If at home plate you have much faith, but your base knowledge is of the straight and narrow, you may just find yourself lost in the left field of creed encumbrance, lordly obstinacy, or pedantic pedagoguery.

Bead 93

If at home plate you have much devotedness and persistence, but your basal preparation and oral training are found to be lacking, you may just find yourself lost in the left field of unconscious error, flawed divergence, or sadly, in the sandtrap of distasteful inaccuracy.

The Ten Ways to Stray from Home Plate, Get Off Base and Find Yourself Lost in Left Field

Bead 94

If at home plate you have not scraped off the artificial mental coatings and additional veneers of all false perceptual appearances, and that the base color of the world as it is, stays covered over with the personality paint of added delusionary appanage, you may just find yourself lost in the left field of dead-end meditations and cul-de-sac contemplations, psychically cornered and overshadowed by an unseen, and unseeing wall of obscuring ignorance.

Bead 95

If at home plate you don't slide in through the dust of delusion and bring to that sacred base the experience of a deep spiritual practice and an intuitive understanding, you may just find yourself lost in the left field of a professional holy hypocrisy, a vain spiritual expertise and a masterly-mendacious nonchalance.

The Ten Ways to Stray from Home Plate, Get Off Base and Find Yourself Lost in Left Field

Bead 96

If at home plate you have not realized the perfect modality of skillful means in the ways and byways of enlightened compassion, you may just find yourself lost in the left field of one of the lesser vehicles of philosophical propinquity, and will thus be treading, inadvertently, upon an inferior pathway.

Bead 97

If at home plate you have not, through mind training and self-initiation, sweated forth the Great Emptiness, you may just find yourself lost in the left field of samsaric sandtraps, and other stray cats.

The Ten Ways to Stray from Home Plate, Get Off Base and Find Yourself Lost in Left Field

Bead 98

If at home plate you don't knock down to size and cork the eight pop bottles of worldly commonplace concerns, you may just find yourself lost in the left field of the commonplace world, outrageously extolling the important rubbish of the usual stuff of life.

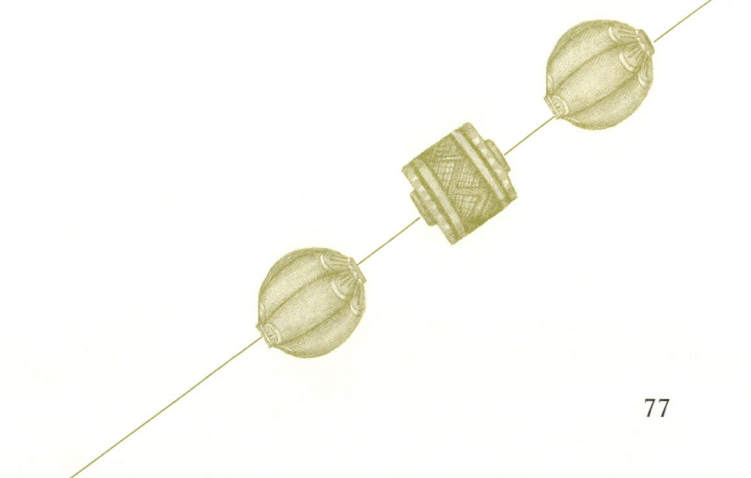

Bead 99

If at home plate you are a respected spiritual star and gather about you your devoted fans, as well as an admiring crowd, you may just find yourself lost in the left field of forever having to please the peanut gallery.

The Ten Ways to Stray from Home Plate, Get Off Base and Find Yourself Lost in Left Field

Bead 100

If at home plate you have developed powerful siddhis and your bat swing is virtuously strong, but your spirit is unstable and your spiritual knees are shaky, you may just find yourself in the left field of becoming a super star of graceful gorgeous swings and stylized strikes, and of supersonic hits and impressive *foul balls*, that 'pow' powerfully hypnotic in the ears of the friendly fans.

These then are the constituted end of the listed **"Ten Ways to Stray from Home Plate, Get Off Base and Find Yourself Lost in Left Field"**.

Mahamudra-Dzogchen Notes 10

Simhananda's
Contemporary, Contemplative Commentaries on the
TENTH SET of Ten Beads of Gampopa's Root Text

Thematically entitled: **The Ten Deviations or Desultory Wanderings to Avoid, Evade, or Shy Away from, whilst Peregrinating upon the PATH**

Simhananda Commentaries 111-120
(In correlation with Gampopa's Mini Mala 10, Beads 91-100)

Simhananda's Contemporary Contemplative Commentary
111

What good is it to be a king of knowledge, yet a pauper in compassionately applied wisdom.

What juicy-fruit goodness, or real demonstrable wisdom, can ever come out of unapplied knowledge, (even if great).

What good is a gorgeous yummy chocolate cake, or a luscious-looking apple pie, if all you do is intellectualize about how good it looks, and you just have to write down the recipe, or better still, memorize it... so that you can reproduce it anytime and set it up in a tidy row on your extra-long, impeccable marble kitchen counter... all one hundred and eight precise and precious yummy pieces.

Intellectual knowledge, whether it be of Buddhist philosophy, or on any subject whatsoever, can be mentally stimulating, or informatically exciting for the consciousness, but ultimately, it remains dry stuff.

And incredibly intellectual knowledge with brilliant understanding is... even drier stuff.

The Ten Deviations or Desultory Wanderings to Avoid, Evade, or Shy Away from whilst Peregrinating upon the PATH

C. C. C. 111-2

In fact, the more that the usually cunning and concrete lower mind understands, the more of a frustrated rift is set up, often unconsciously, but always, (perplexedly), between the head and heart.

Sometimes, the psychic gap and psychological distance existing between these two spiritually strategic centres is plaintively sad, and the ivory-tower syndrome, or the inner solitude which is experienced, is heartrending.

What likely good is it to have a salient series of umpteen, notable degrees and a ton of scholarly written papers on the sutras and tantras of both exoteric and esoteric Buddhism, if you have not yet met the personified Buddha on the dharma road, nor in the inner sanctum of your own heart... where secret initiation truly takes place.

Being a big talker and long on theory, even if it does seem like deep stuff, does not impress a knower of the Buddha. It only seems like deep stuff because the original texts, whether they were written by a Nagarjuna, a Candrakirti, an Atisha, a Gampopa, a Tsongkhapa, a Buton, or a Rendawa... had realized in his own heart, a trained initiatory depth, based on a stabilized attainment of emptiness, and the skillful means of an unequivocally applied wisdom.

C. C. C. 111-3

A good, even brilliant translation of a book on Buddhist philosophy that has great depth of knowledge and even greater wisdom, may make the translator look good, and of course, it may even be a precious contribution to the world of knowledge, and may be at this very moment in the process of being translated and made available to those who speak in only their own language, whether it be French, English, Spanish, Italian, German or any other language, but it is not good work to assume that because you have read, or even translated, such a literary treasure, you are by direct association, or identification, the recipient of the mind-boggling 'innate wisdom' contained therein.

In other words, the electrifying power and blissful juiciness of the very complex kundalini shakti current which literally shakes the tree of the spine, (together with its roots, trunk, limbs, leaves and fruit), which upon arising, stirs and awakens the chakras... and moves the whole heart into a transformed world perception of fiery integration and illumined Wisdom... is usually starkly absent in the mere mental, intellectual approach to the acquisition of Higher Knowledge.

The Ten Deviations or Desultory Wanderings to Avoid, Evade, or Shy Away from whilst Peregrinating upon the PATH

C. C. C. 111-4

Otherwise stated, it is found that in nearly every case, profound and perpetual Dharma practice is the essential element, or key parameter, which is sorely missing.

Consequently, if the student, or scholar, is purely intellectual, or principally mentally-polarized, he is bound to remain but a classy worm of dubitable wisdom, in a shiny can of consciousness that has no essential earth, nor humectant grass, to render his incarnational sojourn sweetly humid and sincerely humble.

Anyhow, who in his right mind would want a dried-up, non-squirming worm as bait for Wisdom. Very few intellectuals actually get caught on the Buddha's fishing pole.

Mind, whether it is the intellectual analytical mind, or the contemplative mind, the insightful mind, the discriminating mind, the worldly wisdom mind, or one of other (numerous) sophic minds, or even one of the emptiness minds… they all must have the mandatory blessings of the golden glint in the Buddha's eye, if a life of true knowledge is to be unequivocally enjoyed, and if such a life is to efficiently serve all sentient beings.

Decidedly, of what beneficial good is it to be a king of knowledge, yet a pauper of applied, compassionate Wisdom.

C. C. C. 112

In starting a sojourn, it is of course, important to know the approximate whereabouts, or at least, the general direction, in which you are going — else, you may just wander about anywhere, or nowhere in particular, and waste everybody's time and energy, not to mention your own.

And it is important to know something about how you are going to get there — else you may never start, nor even, have an intuition as to how long it might take you to reach your nirvanic goal, or destined liberation.

Concomitantly, it is important to have an idea of what to aim for, as well as being cognizant of what spiritual sadhana you are presently doing, and the underlying reasons why — for then, the problem that poses itself to you, is how are you to know other than through some 'direct experience', what ought to be done in undertaking a new practice, or a more advanced study; and perhaps, what ought *not* to be done, and therefore, is to be avoided at all costs, on account of the potentially perturbing, and possibly detrimental effect, it can have upon your enlightened practice.

The Ten Deviations or Desultory Wanderings to Avoid, Evade, or Shy Away from whilst Peregrinating upon the PATH

C. C. C. 112-2

Faith and belief, though useful (at first), are not nearly enough, nor have they ever been insightful enough, to bring someone all the way to supreme realization. Ordinarily, these twin conceptualizers can bring you a pseudo-blissful, mystical feeling, peppered with a superficially beatific experience, but bottom line baby, you stay blind.

Faith and belief as loyal friends, are subtly programmed to constrict the consciousness; they are prone to close you down, or put a subtle, almost airtight lid, upon the progressive deepening of the true Path. They tend, in general, to impede a just apprehension of things genuinely spiritual; or trammel a true understanding of reality 'as it is'.

Everything in faith and belief is more or less relegated to the mystical and mysterious; and to an almost purblind trust that everything will come out all right, if only you keep 'plugging away'.

A whole mountain of fundamental faith and a half-jar full of sophisticated worldly insight do not go far up the celestial ladder leading to Buddhahood, nor even close, to Tushita heaven.

C. C. C. 112-3

A mountain of faith often acts upon the consciousness sometimes, as solidified, or petrified, lazy thought; and there is the danger that it could landslide and crush the subtly fine, crystal-like, celestial step-ladder, leading to Sukhavati.

A half-jar full of sophisticated worldly insight won't give you enough essential energy to climb but the first few fundamental steps of the sacred mount of compassionate comprehension, before your so-called prodigal profundity plainly peters out.

The Ten Deviations or Desultory Wanderings to Avoid, Evade, or Shy Away from whilst Peregrinating upon the PATH

C. C. C. 113

Guru is there to instruct, guide and kick ass... and it's probably the reason why in his spiritual body he wears pointy, shiny cowboy boots.

A disciple must be willing to be Dharma-forged by his Lama Lord.

The guidance of the Guru is especially needed in the beginning stages; and also, in the difficult and extremely subtle, last completion stages; and, of course, in the middle stages where there are so many possible ways to go wrong.

Even after relative enlightenment, the Guru will yeomanly stand by the disciple in the shadows, in case something goes amiss; or, whenever his cowboy boots may be most sorely needed, or dearly missed.

All fun aside, although Guru is technically, our own clear-seeing enlightened Self, he remains in his bodily form a paternal Guide, a most precious gift, and blessed benefit on the Dharma Path.

C. C. C. 113-2

Without an authentically qualified Master Instructor, how is anyone capable, or even able to directly know how to fly his awareness aeroplane toward the lofty, unknown heights of consciousness, much less, indeed, get it correctly off the ground.

It is an almost impossible task to accomplish, without proper training in what to do and how to do it; and what not to do, and how to refrain from doing it; and of what happens or may happen, when you do this, or try that; and if you want to, (or is it wise to), ride out such and such, an inner turbulence which will probably be of this explicit type, or another definite type, depending on the particular practice you have undertaken, at such and such a height, or depth, or profundity of contemplative absorption; and of course, how to clearly interpret, or read accurately with a correct understanding, the varied levels of the abstrusely definable, progressive stages, of the unerring occult path towards Enlightenment.

The Ten Deviations or Desultory Wanderings to Avoid, Evade, or Shy Away from whilst Peregrinating upon the PATH

C. C. C. 113-3

And to be aware, or to beware of this; and watch out for that possibility, or probability of experience; and if this happens, then what to do, to counteract it.

And do we eject, or project, the mind, or the consciousness, to this level of generated awareness; or do we ride this one out to its terminal point of abstraction, which is... "no, never mind, see for yourself and come back to me later when you have achieved and stabilized such and such a state of awareness, and then we'll talk about it some more."

"However, for now, let's take up this point of contentious comprehension, or let us go onwards to the following stage of practical theory..." Etcetera, etcetera.

Without exhaustive flight training from the Chief Pilot Instructor, (that is to say, the Lama Lord), the dangers of doing a wrong maneuver, or making a false move, or even of taking a faulty flight route, are multiple... even if you are well installed in your trainee's seat, and have your aspirational bodhi-belt tightly tied.

C. C. C. 113-4

One wrong move and you tilt dangerously.

Two wrong moves and you almost lose control.

Three wrong moves and you go down!

It is good to be your own best motivational navigator on the path of Mahamudra Practice, but wise it is to remember the need for proper, (and timely), instruction; therefore, be humble enough to allow the Master Pilot to pilot you.

Let not your pride, (or stupidity), of private solo flight fantasies, get the best of you, and be the surreptitious cause of your inevitable crash, (or foolish loss, or dramatic downfall), on the Path.

The Ten Deviations or Desultory Wanderings to Avoid, Evade, or Shy Away from whilst Peregrinating upon the PATH

C. C. C. 114

To be crudely succinct and to make a point which packs a pow, let us simply say that in order to acquire cold clarity, you've got to at all costs, cut through the mystical crap.

If you don't succeed to cut cleanly through, you get a case of 'crappy consciousness', as a conditioned, delusionary dis-ease of existence... and you sit (meditatively) on the toilet bowl of relative reality, and remain in darkness.

The disciple must understand perfectly that which he is spiritually undertaking and mindfully intergrating, under a competent Master.

If perchance, he does not and is lackadaisical in not revealing this form of precarious impasse to his Instructor, then the Buddha mind, or supreme realization, will always elude him.

In the first forays of serious, (but still struggling), discipleship, practice can easily become faulty and flighty, thereby eventuating in the creation of a subtly growing confusion and the erection of egoically darkening walls. The Path itself could be accosted by a merciless array of accrescent encounters of seemingly endless cul-de-sacs. Indeed, in any such period of trying times, spiritual progress can patently, perilously, be upended.

C. C. C. 114-2

Failure to understand the steps, states, and stages on the Path, one by one, as they should outflow, or inflow, into Practice naturally, eventually leads to a complete failure of sounding the true depths of Emptiness; and subsequently, it bequeaths upon the student a minimal chance of integrating the Void, which in turn, insures his failure and frustration, in attaining the ultimate goal of Liberation.

And so, despairing and confused, although he may still feign a certain pride of accomplishment, a frustrated disillusioned, (sometimes darkly-transformed), now mediocre disciple continues to err.

He often, (although quite unconsciously), re-places upon his shoulders his timeless bag of ignorance, thereby symbolizing the retaking of the route of errancy in the lower cycles of existence... for yet another "x" number of trips around the samsaric circle of transgressive living.

The Ten Deviations or Desultory Wanderings to Avoid, Evade, or Shy Away from whilst Peregrinating upon the PATH

C. C. C. 114-3

If a disciple's inherent Innateness has not been personally palmed, and his intrinsic nature still remains paradoxically strange to him, there perdures a definite danger unbeknownst to the delusioned disciple, that the world of apparent phenomenon and relative appearance, (whether illusively ordinary or falsely cosmic), is still apt to reign in his consciousness, (with a tyrannical smile).

If, however, the deviant disciple keeps on passionately, spiritually 'plugging', the devious illusion of a false, (lowly and temporary), freedom, may arise as a mirage within his fixed mind; and the delusional thought of an imagined attainment, or even of a high enlightenment, (which often crystallizes into a set conviction), may sadly and besettingly, come to the illusory fore.

In view of the above statements about how things can go rightfully wrong, it would benefit all students to carefully study the following postulated chain of possible cognitive error to be found, in seriously undertaking the practice of the gradual path to Enlightenment.

C. C. C. 114-4

Mishearing, or malobservation often leads to → misinterpretation, (or mistranslation), leading to → misjudgment → misrendering and → misapplication; and thereby to → mispractice and misappropriation (of the Path) → which may subsequently lead to spiritual misconduct and the → misuse (of siddhis) → and thereon, to a thespian misrepresentation of Attainment.

Darkness, (thus) prevails.

The Ten Deviations or Desultory Wanderings to Avoid, Evade, or Shy Away from whilst Peregrinating upon the PATH

C. C. C. 115

There is no one as pretentious as a self-proclaimed preceptor, or an established-by-other, pro; and this is so on any subject, in any domain, any specialty, and especially so, in the sphere of spirituality.

The spiritual pro's mantra is yep, I 'know this, know that', but rarely does he say 'done this, done that'; or if he does (dare) declaim this, it may be wise to take it with a grain of salt because he really means, 'tried this for a tat, tried that for a tit', since he knows in his heart of hearts that most of his 'doings' have, in reality, deploringly little, or no, actual depth.

Theorists are usually dire letdowns when it comes to the nitty-gritty results of personally demonstrating the practical aftermaths of their, (ought to have been applied first), wisdom-knowledges.

In other words, they cannot contemplate forth, nor cough up in consciousness, the reality of their (professed) understandings.

C. C. C. 115-2

They, (the theorists), usually speak fast, or at a smoothly-clipped pace, eruditely and seemingly without end; and they usually do so with the obvious, subtle pride of a pandit's (profound) knowledgeability; and they (surreptitiously) wish, and want to leave a definite impression on their listeners, that they are, indeed, in the elite class of 'knowers' on the matter.

Ergo, however perceptively erudite they might project to be, either in their stimulating information, or specialized knowledges, which often seem, (usually spontaneously), to *almost* come out of nowhere, rest assured, that this is precisely where they leave you, exactly 'nowhere'... but leaving behind them an impression of 'otherwise'.

In the theorist, there is no real **roar** of Enlightenment, no enlightened **thunderbolt,** no definite **thunderclap** displaying to the inner self of the hearer, the true **seal** of a superior mind apprehending Reality (directly)... straight as a swift arrow, knowing its sure way into the soft, implosive emptiness of the Absolute.

The Ten Deviations or Desultory Wanderings to Avoid, Evade, or Shy Away from whilst Peregrinating upon the PATH

C. C. C. 115-3

Some theory is fine, but it is ultimately, dry stuff (for the humid Heart); and if drawn out too long, (without juicy practice), then the symptoms of contemplative constipation, (or constipatory contemplation), quickly sets in.

Much of all expounded theory comes out of the crystallized, conceptual mind, which has diligently, (intellectually) studied, and which mind has often memorized the cognitive concepts that have been expertly written down, in philosophical treatises and varied commentaries by the past realized, great meditation masters, in their deliberating and delineating out, the subtle intricacies of the progressive path to Enlightenment.

Instead of Buddhahood, jaded scholars have only succeeded in placing a hood over (the) Buddha. They have merely succeeded in slyly mentalizing the intricacies of the multiple mind states, instead of inwardly living them out into personal existence.

Hit the manufactured monks hard on their monk hats and their minds go mad, or suddenly blank, (out of shock to their overweening arrogance); or insult them snappily and they retaliate offensively, demonstrating a lack of mastery over the (emotional) 'kleshas'.

C. C. C. 115-4

Without exception, the wise practitioner, (if he has been well trained), quickly and fastidiously tests out pertinent information, or new knowledge, almost immediately, or directly, after its reception.

The agitated, intellectual, analytical mind is like a gaping mental mouth that knows no satisfaction of intake. If its demagoguery, greed, yearning, or hunger is not countered, nor balanced by a correct contemplative absorption, which calms the spirit and brings a much needed post-meditative equipoise, then it may never be satiated. The mind will always feel unfilled, and unfulfilled.

The scholarly, unappeased mind will always desire more and more intellectual satisfaction, and will literally gorge itself on more and more information and knowledge, to chew and munch on, until an addiction (resembling) mental bulimia sets in… and thus, the scholarly, brilliant regurgitation and the taking-in again, of another surplus of mental foodstuff.

The Ten Deviations or Desultory Wanderings to Avoid, Evade, or Shy Away from whilst Peregrinating upon the PATH

C. C. C. 115-5

Nearly bursting at its mental seams, the over-exerted intellectual, analytical mind will soon self-create a special pair of suspenders that will unconsciously serve a double function — one, to keep a reign upon the tired, bloated heavings of mental excessiveness; and the other, for the suspension, (or rather, the suspending), of the onset of true Wisdom... primarily on account of pride of knowledge and spiritual superficiality... which, as a matter of natural course, will tend to collate (mere) knowledge with (actual) practice, and use this as proof of the authenticity of the mind's projected pudding of (simulated) Realization.

Too much mental 'spiritual expertise' without the disciplined practice of sadhana coupled to Guru guided meditation, deep contemplation and tranquil after-poise, actually dulls, weakens, or rigidifies the ordinary mind... from the unified point of view of Higher Mind.

C. C. C. 115-6

It is good to put into solid practice what Guru or Lama says, before chomping on another piece of meaty esoteric information, in the name of dubious Wisdom.

What's the use of chewing, chewing, and chewing on bits of luscious knowledge, if you never really get to taste it, swallow it, and assimilate its essence.

Inherently, this bad habit of mind is a (self-conceited) waste!

Know that the price of (subtle) pride in the buddhafields of 'spiritual expertise' is high, especially if you hear it and like what you hear, and go for more — without trying it on for possible, or potential, ego impact and supra-consciousness suitability.

Do not take the high and dry road leading to an overdose of brain cell stimulation and superficially deep, haughty thinking, and eventual atmic consciousness paralysis... intimating a spiritually engramic crystalization, a sort of bedeviled vaingloriness... and a sure roller coaster ride down the Dharma path to spiritual perdition... thinking highly all the while, that you are on the high road to constructive consciousness evolution, and a sustainable evolutionary spirituality.

Take rather, the low and wet (contemplative) road to practical, enlightened experience on the Dharma path to spiritual Liberation.

The Ten Deviations or Desultory Wanderings to Avoid, Evade, or Shy Away from whilst Peregrinating upon the Path

C. C. C. 116

The mental disposition of the disciple is of foremost importance on the Higher Mind path of selfless service and ultimate freedom.

The Bodhisattva stance of ecumenistic compassion and equitable love directed towards all sentient beings is unequivocal.

The Bodhisattva position is not one of self-reflection but of other-consideration.

The Bodhisattva posture is not one of posturing to self, (and its selfish progress), but one of plunging forward to give others a helping hand, (to help themselves), out of the quagmire of samsara.

The Bodhisattva perspective recognizes that all sentient beings in incarnation suffer, and too many creatures are silent, walking wounds of existence.

And that both, cultivated Bodhisattva compassion and generated insightful Bodhicitta, are twin beneficent balms tending to life's injuries and all earthly malaise.

C. C. C. 116-2

The Bodhisattva situation is simply one of helping to free others, (by personal association and impartial teaching), from the underlying causes of suffering.

The Bodhisattva vision is to save all sentient beings, (including the living planetary body), from wasteful, unmindful suffering and ultimately, to serve and guide every person to his ultimate happiness, well-being and liberation... before one's own.

The Bodhisattva's best ace-in-the-hole is the constant, tender nurturing of the gift of 'bodhicitta' within his being.

True 'bodhicitta' modestly wears the regular robed sleeves of a Bodhisattva's purified desire, of its wishing to attain Buddhahood for the sheer joy of developing only those super knowledges, which are deemed necessary to generate a powerful and true capacity to help others.

The Ten Deviations or Desultory Wanderings to Avoid, Evade, or Shy Away from whilst Peregrinating upon the PATH

C. C. C. 116-3

The Bodhisattva's 'bodhicitta' robe and sleeves, however, have hems which are delicately embroidered with the fine filigree of Wisdom's golden threading, symbolizing the proper discriminative insight and superior sagacity needed to appropriately love, and compassionately help all sentient beings and living creatures, by the most skillful means possible.

In other words, if a Bodhisattva-in-training wishes to free someone, (or something), he understands that he has to *know* how to do so... so that the best 'means' to aid a single individual in a particular situation, or even (to help) a collective entity in a massive event... must be rightly recognized and accurately assessed without a stitch of a doubt, before the suitable or correct approach can be sagely applied.

Inimitable impartiality is imperative to the Bodhisattva life-view, so that Love can love with a caring equity; so that Compassion can care with a charitable breath; so that Joy can bound forth in a truly unbiased service towards all, and this, with a tireless energy and unbounded vigor.

C. C. C. 116-4

The Bodhisattva working formula of 'bodhicitta' includes the two following dimensional perspectives:

An insightful Understanding of

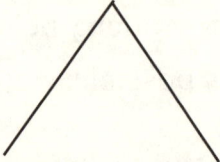

the ingtegral nature of both the phenomenal
and non-dual worlds (in coemergent interdependency)

plus

An authentic Wisdom (state)

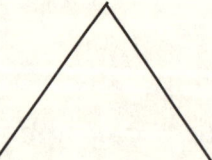

where there is a Real Knowledge of the
Buddha nature, both 'as it is' in Void,
and also, as to how it can be practically applied
to the world of dependent-arising phenomena.

The Ten Deviations or Desultory Wanderings to Avoid, Evade, or Shy Away from whilst Peregrinating upon the PATH

C. C. C. 116-5

Even with arduous discipline and the best of sadhanas, it has always been recognized that without the conscious cultivation of compassionate understanding and the development of skillfully applied 'bodhicitta'... 'bodhisattvaship' has always been considered in danger of being compromised.

Also, commonly acknowledged on the Bodhisattva Path, is the recognition of the psychic cloak of all lesser attainments, and the categorical shame felt regarding all inferior motivation, as inevitably engaging or encouraging, the cloying of the consciousness to a material spirituality, and its clinging to an apparent phenomenology, (and relative reality)... thereby, the beclouding of the mind.

C. C. C. 117

Void, which is the essential nature of the BUDDHA, plus the replete Emptiness of all (relative) impurities, must in a first approach and apprehension, be studied, analyzed, reflected upon and meditated.

In a later, more direct apprehension and with greater experiential comprehension, the Buddha Nature must be seized directly and be occultly understood, before enjoining it to the consciousness, as an integrated constancy of Awareness.

If the inherent non-existence of the Self fails to be firmly fathomed by the mind, then the false 'I' will continue to rule the existential life without reprise — and the five 'kleshas', (defilements of the mind, or poisons of the personality), will be in the passion mode of expression.

The egoic idea that 'I' want (my) happiness above all and that the good things of life are indeed, my due — gives birth to the dynamics of incessant yearning and unceasing desire.

The Ten Deviations or Desultory Wanderings to Avoid, Evade, or Shy Away from whilst Peregrinating upon the PATH

C. C. C. 117-2

If 'I' cannot have this, or that, for my security and comfort, and arr-gh, it has to be done my way, or else — gives birth to frustration, impatience and lots of anger.

'I' do not like 'this' at all, but yes, 'that' is good (for me) — gives birth to the egoic erection of a persona-propped mechanism, which features a polarized attraction-repulsion dichotomy.

'I', self-important that 'I am', and with all the due attention (from others) that 'I' should be getting, because 'me-thinks' secretly that 'I' am the best — gives birth to arrogance, vanity and pride.

'I', and heaven forbid that some other 'I' is just as good, or perhaps better than 'I' am; or that he has more of this, or that; and heaven forbid, that someone is out to outclass me, or already has, (in his possession), what by all rights should have been mine — gives birth to envy, rivalry, resentment, and jealousy.

So these, in summary, are the five 'kleshas' that bear down upon the existential 'I', and demand their pound of real flesh from what is found to be fundamentally, a phenomenal shadow.

C. C. C. 117-3

These 'kleshas' seem to have a beyond death sway over the (ordinary) consciousness, and they somehow, (by trick or treat), succeed to enslave the pure awareness, which becomes a despairing, but willing prisoner, of the ensnaring circularity of samsaric life.

Being incarcerated in this enticing incarnational jail, the 'awareness-mind' is not liable to a karmic parole any day soon, and Freedom for most of sentient beings, remains today, as yesterday, but a far-off dream.

Existential life, indeed, is a sinister trickster and within its circle and cross, it seriously means to keep man's Divinity, humanly bound.

The human ego spawns dependent-arising upon the existence of an 'I', within the illusionary world of bipolarized phenomena, which also spontaneously-arises pendent upon a mixture of provisional parameters and contingent clauses.

It is interesting to discover then, that as individualized awareness unfolds, the ego itself grows very subtle, and the ante of the game for ultimate Liberation, goes up.

The Ten Deviations or Desultory Wanderings to Avoid, Evade, or Shy Away from whilst Peregrinating upon the Path

C. C. C. 117-4

How is this process engaged?

By the nefarious creation of a certain wishful ideation, or creative dream aspect of the consciousness, which consists principally of a significantly self-sensitized portion of the personality, or a psychic projection of the subtle ego, to which esoteric nomenclature has aptly given the dubitable appellation of *spiritual ego.*

It goes without saying that the aforementioned pseudo-spiritualizing process, and all other false progress attributed to the so-called 'spiritualizing of the ego', is a dangerous game to play... and it does usually end up as the raving epitome of delusional blindness... but a very important eagle feather it is, in the cap of all spurious and factitious mindsets.

One cannot realistically go too far upon the path of Liberation, and toward a spiritually scientific reality of freeing others, (usually an astral dream), if one is still a prisoner of the idea of a shadow self being identified with, as the 'I' am, or 'I' exist.

C. C. C. 117-5

Wherever and whenever there is an 'I', we also find crazy (consciousness) glue, in existential abundance.

Stuck to cyclic samsara, and knowing little-or-nothing about any of the nine absorptions and the various empties, the no-thingness void, or the full-essence voidness, of the true Buddha Nature... it becomes obviously clear that true clarity, (or real transparency), signifying the capacity to see things as they really are in their Basic Inherency, is more than apt, to be substantially missing.

And if this is so, the spiritual practitioner, no matter what self-initiated and ambitious practices he may have undertaken, will in all probability and without ever having a clue, remain exactly where he is... that is, peddling away on his spiritual bicycle, (with wheels fractionalizing away in hot air), and himself smugly seated on a dais of some subtle, intellectualized, ego trip.

The Ten Deviations or Desultory Wanderings to Avoid, Evade, or Shy Away from whilst Peregrinating upon the PATH

C. C. C. 117-6

Such a disciple will remain in his hearts of hearts, spiritually delusional, in that the only real progress he will be making is that of the 'spiritual ego' stating its case, and thinking that it is going full-steam ahead forward, towards Liberation... which, of course, only means more of the 'I' crystallization and the further hardening of the salt of consciousness... into all sorts of artificial, granulated, dependently-arising, apparently evolving phenomena.

Invariably, it is up to each disciple to either, plant his mind firmly in the rich Buddha soil of the Great Emptiness, or else, choose to foolishly plant it in the unstable, ever-shifting quicksands of cyclically evolving samsara.

It is his choice, and ultimately, your move.

C. C. C. 118

Absolutely nothing in the outer world will bring you lasting satisfaction, and even less, lasting happiness.

Once you hook the mind's interest, (that is, when your mind bites into the red rubber ball of an idea, belief, or objective), be it the desire for peace, calm or comfort; security, happiness or well-being; or just the wish to live the opposite of what you have actually been living as a karmic condition, (or lesson of life), with its non-acceptance thereof — or even, just the simple desire for the accumulation of material objects and material gain, fame and what not... it is imperative for the sadhaka to know that the mind, (of its own inherent tendency), if not checked or neutralized in its forward tumbling motion, will gather momentum and automatically want more and more of what it already has, or thinks it has not... and in wanting what it has not, will ironically produce just more of what it already has... for example, misery, unhappiness, and more suffering.

The Ten Deviations or Desultory Wanderings to Avoid, Evade, or Shy Away from whilst Peregrinating upon the Path

C. C. C. 118-2

Complexity, without a strong base of simplicity supporting it and encircling it, makes for an always thinking mind and agitated spirit.

And with the common mind's multitude of wants and prejudices, personal predilections and atmospheric moods, emotional see-saws and overall attitudinal dispositions, it would be easy to see, (if only there was a heedful halt), how the basic life philosophy of a person, (which is a conglomerate of all the above-mentioned factors), influences or attracts, situations and events to him which can bear either, the seal of plain positivity, or the stamp of noticeable negativity.

This commentary is perhaps not the place to elaborate on the four worldly pairs of antipathetic sympathies — that is to say, those of pleasure/pain, gain/loss, praise/blame and fame/infamy. However, the major point to be made regarding these passionate antipathies is that they all stem from, or have their roots, in mind *wanting* the best and the most for the delusional 'I', (that sense or notion of 'ego-self'), that spontaneously and unconsciously arises, as the false personality, (framed in existential technicolor).

C. C. C. 118-3

And riding upon the personality's coattail, is the dilemma of the shadow-self's confused attachment toward the perceptually appropriated, but definitely self-christened, samsaric pairs of positive and negative polarization.

The student must clearly comprehend that all discomfort, discontent and dissatisfaction, which have to do with the 'eight worldly concerns', (mentioned priorly), are already at once and in the same expressed breath, mind-made and desire-fed.

These altered, fabricated states of consciousness do not exist on their own.

However, when these states are activated by an arising sense of self, selectively and willfully wishing forth, (something or other), know then, that the sky is the limit concerning need and want.

For instance, at what point in the spectrum of the continuous mind-flow of consciousness, does gain turn into greed... which goes counter-clockwise to what one should really feel, if only gratitude, (rather than greed), would rise naturally, to meet our already met needs.

The Ten Deviations or Desultory Wanderings to Avoid, Evade, or Shy Away from whilst Peregrinating upon the PATH

C. C. C. 118-4

How blessed are we in multifarious ways and know it not, nor do we savor a glowing gratitude in the heart, and this simply because the blind mind has the (perverted) tendency to focus on what it does not have, or wishes that it had.

Thuswise, the mind's unabated agitation. Whence, its eternal dissatisfaction. Thuswise, its constant (state of) discontentment. Whence, its unresolved, persistent lack of fulfillment.

Unhappiness happens first in the mind; it is a mind-generated state (of affairs); an internal mental condition.

Unhappiness rises up in the mind and permutes the atmospheric webbing of the evolving consciousness based on the simple fact, (and unwise act), of the non-acceptance of what is transpiring in (one's) life regarding the particular lesson to be learned, or the singular wisdom to be heard.

C. C. C. 118-5

There are far too many professionals of unhappiness today, propagating attitudes of complaint and platitudes of discontent; and feeding antinomic feelings of questionable indignation, or even prompting outright dissatisfaction; and giving permission, in the holy cause of self-expression, to rampant emotions of overt, (or subtle), negativities, and therefore, of indiscriminately encouraging lives of unwarranted unhappiness and unnecessary misery.

Most of it is based, of course, on personally biased misconceptions of life's basic needs, and to the general (fundamental) lack of discerning worldly wisdom, regarding what is felt, (or believed to be), the main ingredients, or essential elements, of what makes up true happiness.

A mind replete with gratitude is a mind naturally disposed to meditation... that is, content to repose in its natural calm state of existential gratefulness.

The Ten Deviations or Desultory Wanderings to Avoid, Evade, or Shy Away from whilst Peregrinating upon the Path

C. C. C. 118-6

If you place your mind's focus, or its attentive power upon your unhappiness, miscontent, or (overly-imagined) misery, then the predisposed processional march of such alike-automated thoughts will follow suit, and the subjective themes that will most likely pass by 'film-like' in your consciousness, will be those of a forever elusive happiness, and of agglutinative feelings which may be atmospherically qualified as 'dukka-like' adjuncts, fully saturated with moody mind-sets such as sadness, anxiety, heaviness and hurt; and earmarked by passive-aggressive emotions bearing the recognizable marks of repressed anger, resentment and bitterness; and damaged by scars and wounds often inflicted by one's own close relatives and loved ones... and ergo, the curse of samsaric circularity continues on and on.

All object-oriented attainment and material gain which is aggressively secured, may indeed get you what you (think) you want in life, as far as worldly elegance and non-sacred ornateness are concerned... but all such garish garnishment, from the perspective of the innate simplicity of Spirit, is regarded to be no more than mere ornamental wastage, and therefore, considered conspicuously unnecessary.

C. C. C. 118-7

The whole garish, material rigmarole and silly ring-around-a-rosy, mind-busy appanage is envisoned to be a burden to life's simple joys... for no greater joy is there than Life Itself being simply and artfully what It Is, in your life — right now.

Why desire more than the pow-or-wow of the *Now* blessing you, and just being the healing balm of this moment's Buddhamind, earthly touching you.

The Ten Deviations or Desultory Wanderings to Avoid, Evade, or Shy Away from whilst Peregrinating upon the PATH

C. C. C. 119

Before an audience to which you are about to speak, perhaps on the subject of Dharma, be innerly sure that the Dharma rules you, and not the audience, you.

To whomsoever you are about to speak and who desires to learn about Dharma, and who wishes to lean upon the Dharma, if your attitude is humble, respectful and receptive, then you will be forthly inspired, (often by your personal Yidam), to speak the right word, construct the right sentence, convey the right idea and introduce the right theme, for the particular group of hearers before you.

You will not be tempted to talk about what the people in the audience, perhaps in their ignorance or suffering, feel, wish, or think they want, (or think they need) to hear, in order to justify, or corroborate the existential corral of their basic physical reality... that is, their existential Okayness with what is going on in their lives right now.

In so doing, you will simply be saying, without any outward pretense, or untoward ostentation, what the Buddhamind within you, spontaneously dictates.

C.C.C. 119-2

All will be said effortlessly, in such a skillful way that will be judged appropriate to the consciousness of the audience, and which will be proper to the hour.

If you have great faith in the Dharma and trust your Buddhamind, you will find everything within you to heed and meet the moment's needs.

Rest assured, the consciousness of the collective all, will be sensitively touched and deeply moved by you. Each and every individual will in all probability have his (personal) question, or dilemma (of the moment), answered in a most wonderful and reflective way.

Therefore, do not strive to please people, but please the Buddha within you as you speak; thuswise, the event, the environment and the people, will as one be blessed, and all will receive grace.

Strive otherwise, and you merely kowtow to the common mind.

The Ten Deviations or Desultory Wanderings to Avoid, Evade, or Shy Away from whilst Peregrinating upon the PATH

C. C. C. 120

Ignorant people are facilely impressed and easily manipulated. This is so because of their almost total identification with the notion of the 'I' as self, and by extension, therefore, of egoic existence... this being their primary source of sensual experience, and sensational exploration.

Common people, because of their mean mind and concretized consciousness, as well as their addictive dependency upon the senses, with their ensuing (limited) explorations and crystallized beliefs, actually do prevent the Buddhamind from coming unto its own, naturally, from deep within them.

In nearly all cases, where the consciousness demonstrates a marked characteristic of closed commonness, the subjective mind's (objective) inner space, which is so rigorously needed for the purposes of expansion, is simply not available.

Instead of a much needed, receptive open-mindedness, a concrete conceptual crystallization actually, (or contractually), takes place.

C. C. C. 120-2

Common people are prone to a literalness of interpretation, and an untested acceptance of what is said, or laid down, (as hypothesis, doctrine, or law), by the so-called authorities, or recognized sources of the religious, (spiritual), political, and scientific communities.

Consequently, in a sort of passive display of misplaced humility, simple folks inadvertently give their power away to the pandits, (scholars and authorities), who seem to know... because they talk, speak and preach so-o-o well... and do puja with such pious application, and proper aptitudinal punch.

The peasant's usually pleasant, pliable mind, which is so easily impressionable by apparent erudition and erudite speakability, is easily susceptible to being led, (or misled), by the expertly facile practitioner upon the Path, who has, (no doubt), perused the scriptures to a certain (limited) depth of understanding.

The Ten Deviations or Desultory Wanderings to Avoid, Evade, or Shy Away from whilst Peregrinating upon the PATH

C. C. C. 120-3

It is, therefore, with serious appraisal, that the following wise counsel is given to all those yet non-matured, 'uncooked' practitioners of the Sacred Way of Dharma: "that they should reflectively and definitely, resist the temptation of going out prematurely on the so-called 'village-circuit' of easy mind suasion, and path persuasion".

Circus performances of acquired personal powers, (called siddhis), all of them very minor when placed within the larger perspective of real Bodhisattva-ship, and the patent overt display and demonstration of sanctimonious moral virtues, (which stink all the way up to Heaven), are a pervasive temptation to all those who are not quite pure enough, (or ready enough), to teach from the Wisdom viewpoint of the Great Perfection.

C. C. C. 120-4

Therefore, if someone immature, incomplete, or imperfect teaches the Dharma just to get the popular applause, fame, or financial support of the plebian proletariat of the simple in spirit, (but often sincere of heart), and whose modest mindset is one of self-depreciation, or low self-esteem... if such a lama, (or Buddhist layman), deliberately sets out to perform such (ignoble) dharmic teaching practices, and thereon, poses as a person of great realization upon the Path... then Maitreya, the Christ Teacher, being a later-born brother of the BUDDHA, was correct in calling such spiritual pariahs, 'pharisees', pretending to be 'pure of heart and poor in spirit'.

Therefore, let all potential instructors abstain from erring in this wayward way, and in being true to the Dharma, let them first, always be true to themselves.

These then, are Simhananda's contemporary, contemplative commentaries regarding **"The Ten Deviations or Desultory Wanderings to Avoid, Evade, or Shy Away from, whilst Peregrinating upon the PATH"**.

Mini Mala XI

The ELEVENTH SERIES of Ten Beads from
Gampopa's Golden Garland

Gampopa Beads 101 to 110

The Ten Delusionary Dilemmas of Man that ought to be
Correctly Cognized and Astutely Apprehended, but can easily get
Mind-Muddled and Mixed-Up, with their Jigsawed
Antipodal Plight, or Genuine Counterpart

Gampopa's Root Text
Bead 101

The first delusionary dilemma of man that ought to be correctly cognized and astutely apprehended, is the relative reality of: 'an individual, or personal desire'... whose false fiction can easily get mind-muddled with its jigsawed antipodal plight, (or genuine counterpart), which, when rightly recognized, is discovered to be the perduring condition of: 'a dispassionate Devotion, or true Faith'.

The Ten Delusionary Dilemmas of Man that ought to be Correctly Cognized and
Astutely Apprehended, but can easily get Mind-Muddled and Mixed-Up,
with their Jigsawed Antipodal Plight, or Genuine Counterpart

Bead 102

The second delusionary dilemma of man that ought to be correctly cognized and astutely apprehended, is the relative reality of: 'a captive passion and affective attachment'... whose false fiction can easily get mind-muddled, or mixed-up, with its jigsawed antipodal plight, (or genuine counterpart), which, when rightly recognized, is discovered to be the perduring condition of: 'an enfired Compassion and a loving Kindness'.

Bead 103

The third delusionary dilemma of man that ought to be correctly cognized and astutely apprehended, is the relative reality of: 'emptiness minded by the ordinary mind'... whose false fiction can easily get mind-muddled, or mixed-up, with its jigsawed antipodal plight, (or genuine counterpart), which, when rightly recognized, is discovered to be the perduring condition of: 'the inherent Emptiness to be found in the raincloud of all knowable things'.

The Ten Delusionary Dilemmas of Man that ought to be Correctly Cognized and Astutely Apprehended, but can easily get Mind-Muddled and Mixed-Up, with their Jigsawed Antipodal Plight, or Genuine Counterpart

Bead 104

The fourth delusionary dilemma of man that ought to be correctly cognized and astutely apprehended, is the relative reality of: 'the existential néant as found in the philosophy of radical nihilism, or that of absolute negation'... whose false fiction can easily get mind-muddled, or mixed-up, with its jigsawed antipodal plight, (or genuine counterpart), which, when rightly recognized, is discovered to be the perduring condition of: 'the primordial Dharmadhatu'.

Bead 105

The fifth delusionary dilemma of man that ought to be correctly cognized and astutely apprehended, is the relative reality of: 'a predisposed dependence upon the relative phenomenon of experience'... whose false fiction can easily get mind-muddled, or mixed-up, with its jigsawed antipodal plight, (or genuine counterpart), which, when rightly recognized, is discovered to be the perduring condition of: 'real Realization, or consummate Accomplishment'.

The Ten Delusionary Dilemmas of Man that ought to be Correctly Cognized and Astutely Apprehended, but can easily get Mind-Muddled and Mixed-Up, with their Jigsawed Antipodal Plight, or Genuine Counterpart

Bead 106

The sixth delusionary dilemma of man that ought to be correctly cognized and astutely apprehended, is the relative reality of: 'pietism, phariseeism, and hypocrisy... allied to such apt sidekicks as mendaciousness, self-righteousness and deceitfulness'... whose false fiction can easily get mind-muddled, or mixed-up, with its jigsawed antipodal plight, (or genuine counterpart), which, when rightly recognized, is discovered to be the perduring condition of: 'Innocence, Clarity and Simplicity, bonded to honesty, righteousness and incorruptibility'.

Bead 107

The seventh delusionary dilemma of man that ought to be correctly cognized and astutely apprehended, is the relative reality of: 'the predicament of the fervently mad monk, (who is plainly off-his-rocker), and who has been partially, or totally compromised, or marred, by Mara'... whose false fiction can easily get mind-muddled, or mixed-up, with its jigsawed antipodal plight, (or genuine counterpart), which, when rightly recognized, is discovered to be the perduring condition of: 'the real McCoy, commonly known on the Dharma path as "the divine fool, crazy guru, or mad lama"... in whom all false paradigms and spiritual balloons have unequivocally collapsed'.

The Ten Delusionary Dilemmas of Man that ought to be Correctly Cognized and Astutely Apprehended, but can easily get Mind-Muddled and Mixed-Up, with their Jigsawed Antipodal Plight, or Genuine Counterpart

Bead 108

The eighth delusionary dilemma of man that ought to be correctly cognized and astutely apprehended, is the relative reality which aptly characterizes: 'the divine deceiver, the smooth swindler, the mesmerizing con man, and beguiling charlatan of false spirituality'... whose false fiction can easily get mind-muddled, or mixed-up, with its jigsawed antipodal plight, (or genuine counterpart), which, when rightly recognized, is discovered to be the perduring condition which circumscribes: 'the genuine yogi, superior seer, and Lama Lord, who is sometimes infamously known, as the inflaming, miracle-making, completely irresistible, Budh Beserker*'.

*Budh Beserker, see page 175.

Bead 109

The ninth delusionary dilemma of man that ought to be correctly cognized and astutely apprehended, is the relative reality of: 'subtle self-will, self-service, self-esteem, self-regard, and self-importance, benefitting mainly, or entirely, the small personal self'... whose false fictiion can easily get mind-muddled, or mixed-up, with its jigsawed antipodal plight, (or genuine counterpart), which, when rightly recognized, is discovered to be the perduring condition of: 'selflessness, self-sacrifice, self-restraint, self-mastery, and finally, self-annihilation... benefitting very obviously, the nondual Other-as-Self — being absolutely, the Notself'.

The Ten Delusionary Dilemmas of Man that ought to be Correctly Cognized and Astutely Apprehended, but can easily get Mind-Muddled and Mixed-Up, with their Jigsawed Antipodal Plight, or Genuine Counterpart

Bead 108

The eighth delusionary dilemma of man that ought to be correctly cognized and astutely apprehended, is the relative reality which aptly characterizes: 'the divine deceiver, the smooth swindler, the mesmerizing con man, and beguiling charlatan of false spirituality'... whose false fiction can easily get mind-muddled, or mixed-up, with its jigsawed antipodal plight, (or genuine counterpart), which, when rightly recognized, is discovered to be the perduring condition which circumscribes: 'the genuine yogi, superior seer, and Lama Lord, who is sometimes infamously known, as the inflaming, miracle-making, completely irresistible, Budh Beserker*'.

*Budh Beserker, see page 175.

Bead 109

The ninth delusionary dilemma of man that ought to be correctly cognized and astutely apprehended, is the relative reality of: 'subtle self-will, self-service, self-esteem, self-regard, and self-importance, benefitting mainly, or entirely, the small personal self'... whose false fictiion can easily get mind-muddled, or mixed-up, with its jigsawed antipodal plight, (or genuine counterpart), which, when rightly recognized, is discovered to be the perduring condition of: 'selflessness, self-sacrifice, self-restraint, self-mastery, and finally, self-annihilation... benefitting very obviously, the nondual Other-as-S<small>ELF</small> — being absolutely, the Notself'.

The Ten Delusionary Dilemmas of Man that ought to be Correctly Cognized and Astutely Apprehended, but can easily get Mind-Muddled and Mixed-Up, with their Jigsawed Antipodal Plight, or Genuine Counterpart

Bead 110

The tenth delusionary dilemma of man that ought to be correctly cognized and astutely apprehended, is the relative reality (paradigm) of: 'masterful self-deception, and the cunning conveying of false skillful means, and calculated stratagems'... whose false fiction can easily get mind-muddled, or mixed-up, with its jigsawed antipodal plight, (or genuine counterpart), which, when rightly recognized, is discovered to be the perduring condition of: 'perceptive self-insight, and the mindful utilization of what is known, as true skillful means, or right stratagems'.

These then are the constituted end of the listed "**Ten Delusionary Dilemmas of Man that ought to be Correctly Cognized and Astutely Apprehended, but can easily get Mind-Muddled and Mixed-Up, with their Jigsawed Antipodal Plight, or Genuine Counterpart**".

Mahamudra-Dzogchen Notes 11

Simhananda's
Contemporary, Contemplative Commentaries on the
ELEVENTH SET of Ten Beads of Gampopa's Root Text

Thematically entitled: The Ten Mix-Ups of Non-Identical Twins
and Their Ensuing Embarrassments

Simhananda Commentaries 121-130
(In correlation with Gampopa's Mini Mala 11, Beads 101-110)

Simhananda's Contemporary Contemplative Commentary
121

"It happens oftentimes, in the spiritual field that the student evinces a projected 'idealized' fixation, vis-à-vis his instructor.

Such a sadhaka may secretly think of his teacher in somewhat the following terms (of endearment):

"He has such a wonderful and godly nature and such impeccable features... a fine face, golden glowing skin, soft flowing hair, a melodious voice, and is graceful of body and limbs. His feet are pure nectar furling the earth, his erudition is unsurpassed, and his wisdom is beyond words, and worlds. His mind pervades the very depths of emptiness, and his clarity is supremely sovereign. His heart overflows with genuine bliss, and he is the epitome of pure compassion incarnate."

"I am but his humble devotee... with heart, soul and spirit entirely devoted to him. I will serve him with all my being, and follow him to the ends of the earth. And I will most certainly join him at my death, and be with him for all eternity, in Tushita Heaven."

Know that this type of devotion clearly spells attachment; no light-minded argument, please.

The Ten Mix-Ups of Non-Identical Twins and Their Ensuing Embarrassments

C. C. C. 121-2

Notice that the main desire kindling the eternal fire in such a disciple's heart is that of imbibing the Master's energy, or being in the auric field, of the Lama's presence at all times; and when, or if, there is a relative period of apartness, then a great missing begins, and the great bird of yearning sets in.

It is a spiritual truism, that real devotion inevitably involves a positive karmic connection, with a Master.

Having this firm, past relational ground of service to the Master under him, the true disciple continues in this lifetime, to impeccably serve in the full trust and complete confidence of his Lama's cause; and he reveres the very ground of his Being, (for being Here); and he strictly adheres to the particular Path and practices, which his Master teaches him will lead to Liberation... and this, for the greater cause and overall benefit of his enlightened Lama's blessings and service, to all sentient beings everywhere.

Such a disciple devotes himself sanely to his Lama Lord, or True Teacher, and his love and duty to him are absolute, unquestionable, and entirely free of any form of 'stickiness'.

C. C. C. 121-3

The steadfast disciple's compliance to duty or to the Dharma, and his wise, (immediate, sensitive and unquestionable), 'occult obedience' to the Lama Lord and his cause, come from habitual practice, and out of the common ground of past training, and spiritual experience.

Oftentimes, it goes beyond the Beyond, to the near nirvanic realms of the authentic Buddha States... thereby underscoring the fundamental ground of Inherent Existence itself, and of applied Bodhisattva-ship, owing to the many kindly graces of his Lama Lord.

The Ten Mix-Ups of Non-Identical Twins and Their Ensuing Embarrassments

C. C. C. 122

True Compassion is both object-less and relationless.

It is what it is, and is likened to the sun which always shines forth its rays of caring, kindness and love upon one and all, irregardless of sex, station, or race.

True Compassion's close, non-identical twin is that of impassioned empathy.

Impassioned empathy, whilst at times closely resembling authentic compassion, remains in the main, attached, partial, and full of self-interest.

Impassioned empathy is primarily personal, impulsively relative, highly selective, and motivationally complex in choosing those few, who are meritorious and worthy, and are therefore, deemed fit to receive the blessings of this present someone's sympathetic attention.

C. C. C. 122-2

True compassion is detached, impartial and unbiased; it is self-possessed, yet remains ever non-subjective and non-identified, and therefore, unswayed.

True compassion is simple, fundamental and entirely giving at all times, in its dispassionate and disinterested egalitarianism.

Some of the more obvious traits to watch for in discriminating a true being of real compassion from a personality who is truly imbued with the characteristics of an impassioned empathy, are to be found in the following clues regarding the latter's delineation.

'Impassioned empathy' has the following (easily) identifiable traits:

- tender feeling and engaged emotionalism

- passionate endeavor for the circumstances of another's happiness and success... that 'other', usually being identified as a personal extension of one's self... for instance, my child, husband, wife, lover, mistress, father, mother, devotee, pupil, etc.

- likableness and likability dependency

- stimulative fascination; feeling real good about someone, or something; sudden arousal (to do good)

C. C. C. 122-3

- addictive desirousness, entanglement, and bondage

- zealousness and fervency outflows; useless and wasteful fretting; an instinctual, or impatient, inclination to help, save, rescue, or redeem someone; or ameliorate the circumstantial, painful conditions, thereof... and bring, (or impose), my stratagem for a peaceful resolution

- prone to subtle, or overt glamors, vis-à-vis the self; and other self-glorifications, vis-à-vis seemingly peaceful, or apparently beneficent, humanitarian aid

- quick to give, quick to take away; exemplifying a take-back tendency

- hearty personalized affection; strong sentimentalism; romantic idealism, and undiscerning devotion

- impercipient but faithful love; unconstrained heart smittenness; bonded physical enthrallment; and having a blind 'soft spot', for such and such a someone, project, or plan

- subtle, or overt demands to be loved, or paid attention to; plus all services rendered to that which has an affective price tag.

C. C. C. 122-4

Any, and all of these, and many more, can equally qualify as salient features which can incarnate an 'impassioned empathy'.

Note them well.

Do not make of true compassion something sentimentally spiritual.

Do not make of real compassion the indiscriminate domain of undiscerning, slipsliding, proviso-proned, passionate fools.

C. C. C. 123

The person who said that 'ignorance is bliss' came very close to the relative truth.

Ordinary, concrete mind, before it sets out and activates itself in its royal regalia gear of knowing 'this' and already knowing 'that'... is, at full restful potential, blissful and reposed in its natural state of 'not knowing'.

This is perhaps why some sham mystics and falsely-realized ones, when they are queried about such and such a particular spiritual practice, or about a special snippet of occult knowledge, reply in a beleaguered bawl, or bothered bellow, something somewhat like: "How should I know!? It just is... that's all!" Or else, empty-headed, blank, disoriented, or disinterested... do not answer at all.

It might be more appropriate to recognize that these wisened, old, con-men, or cool coons, are sending a chill-out message, to those who can (subtly) read between the lines.

C. C. C. 123-2

Their respectable, cosmic, egocentric message goes probably somewhat along the following familiar lines: "That they are at this very precious moment of discourteous questioning, in an absolute at-one-ment state of non-dual, non-differentiated awareness... and do not under any circumstance, wish to leave, nor needlessly break-up, that state of pure emptiness identification... merely to answer a measly, worldly-polarized question, requiring a measly, relatively abstract response."

"In other words, *my* state of Absolute Awareness would have to step back down into the crass consciousness of mere relativity to answer such a question."

"Descent denied... come back later."

The emptiness of the sincere, unrealized man is usually little more than an exalted exercise in lofty reasoning and intuitive logic, accompanied by a simple contemplative analysis of causal (evolutionary) phenomenality... with the all of it undertaken from a perspective, of relatively tranquil absorption, or negative calm, which is often taken, (or rather, mistaken), for real meditational depth.

The Ten Mix-Ups of Non-Identical Twins and Their Ensuing Embarrassments

C. C. C. 123-3

Emptiness is creatively, visually, and astrally-imagined to be, a subtly such-and-such a thought-feeling thing, or even, a stopping of all thought, or inner dialogue, at will.

And a sort of specious, or nominal mental-at-oneness, is then used to secure in mind the (introjected) thought-feeling, or mental inkling, of 'voidness'.

If however, a disciple completely exhausts his mind's analytical foray into duality-based relativity, and the mind itself, being at rope's end, falls completely consumed, (or is extenuated), into a momentary pause of absolute no-thing-ness, or rests into an absorbed, eternal twinkle of truly natural repose... then, the ordinary mind, may just for a moment let go of its stranglehold, upon the concrete consciousness, and may perchance directly apprehend, or directly experience, the innate nature of the Abstract Consciousness... which is made-up essentially of the same stuff as Emptiness, but is being expressed, (or experienced), on a different lower dimensional level, but is still (relatively) known as Higher Consciousness, or Superior Mind.

C. C. C. 123-4

The point which is here being made, is that no matter how brief such a (mind-less) experience of Emptiness is, it is still, (within the space of a blink of an eye), relatively *real*.

It is a momentary, direct apprehension, or true transient absorption of Voidness stuff... and not a thought-fabricated, astrally-imagined, projected idea of (what) emptiness (might look, or be like).

Learn to discern well, therefore, between the two states of consciousness, and mix not the psychically generated ecstacy of a pseudo, essentially feeling-imagined, mentalized state of Void, for the naturally arising Bliss of a full 'At-one-ment of Emptiness'... that is to say, the consciousness experience, or state, no matter how brief, of the 'No-Thing-ness ecstasis of REALITY'.

C. C. C. 124

The Dharmadhatu, that is, the Great Expanse, or Ultimate Openness, which is, also, in common parlance, referred to as the ongoing evolutionary Open-Endedness of all things, is the primal genitive domain of the Adi Buddha.

It is the all-encompassing Eternal Existence, or Life Energy, sometimes related to by the mystic, as the Infinite Consciousness. It is to be descried, or ascertained, within that apparently ever-expanding, Illimitable Immensity, known as Incommensurable Space.

All things that potentially are, spontaneously arise within this unbegotten, aeonian Living Entity, called 'Primordial Space'.

And yet, concomitant with the evolutionary expansion of the never-ending worlds upon worlds of phenomena, the Dharmadhatu, being in cosmic coexistence and co-simultaneity with the phenomenal worlds, Itself undergoes expansion.

Or it all seems to, mainly through the mechanism, or magical modality of the galloping metamorphing Mind, or that part of It, which is the constantly expansive, unremittingly evolutionary Consciousness.

C. C. C. 124-2

All-That-Is Mind voids itself into the Great Void, or into that Inexpressible Everything, which is the inexhaustive Expanse of Emptiness.

Yet, in the same way that a grain of salt melts and merges, as it is dropped into the ocean and seems to disappear, All-That-Is Mind intimately becomes through the sacrifice of its illusionary self, the Infinite Ocean of Void.

This Great Ocean of Emptiness into which all things are absorbed like so many grains of soluble salt, and from which all things again arise spontaneously and simultaneously, is in basic fact, the great Consummate Ocean of Compassion... without which, 'THAT, being the Ultimate Suchness', nothing else could possibly be.

In other words, out of Primordial Nothingness and from Essential Emptiness, rises triumphantly, Exultant Existence.

C.C.C. 124-3

But, as phenomenal existence empties itself continually into the Absolute Void, it becomes consistently, absolutely no-thing at all.

Yet, this ongoing process of the apparent emergence of manifestation in particle and non-particle form, is refreshingly washed and regenerated by its sisyphean emptying.

Moreover, it immediately, simultaneously, unisonously, at this very moment, (because there is no time element involved here), regains the ever present pregnant potential of Being absolutely every-thing all-at-once again, in sequential time, and in its appropriate periodicity of material round, and in the manifestly correct spiraling chain, of evolutionary events.

Therefore, materially and spiritwise, that is, in matter versus spirit, nothing is ever negated, or lost.

There is no nihilistic tendency, to be fundamentally found anywhere, in Inherent Existence.

C. C. C. 124-4

There is only, fully potentized and infinitely potentialized, primal Emptiness, within which no-thing can exist, but out of which the Incomprehensible Cosmic Winds nebulously give birth... first of all, to the great Primordial Silence and co-simultaneously, upon a spontaneously arising Cosmic Breath, there Is... the existential emergence in coextensive fashion, of the birth of the variegated multi-dimensional Heavens, and where, upon the up of the same Celestial Wink, there precipitately, (but naturally), appears the origin of the gross spiritual worlds of material manifestation.

However, there is no nihilism anywhere in all the worlds of manifestation, no radical annihilation of anything created, where the cycle is (usually) that of birth, death and rebirth... where being from life to life, continues via consciousness to expand exuberantly from out of the First Clap of No-Sound, into the state of Natural Being... which once again, must be cyclically re-claimed through the disciple's conscious entering of the Great Void, (or Brimful Emptiness), via Buddhic ENLIGHTENMENT.

C. C. C. 125
(Commentary in four parts)

Part I

On the Dharma path of serious practice, the disciple may have a spiritually ongoing experience of 'blissing out', or of 'being blissed out', for a relative period of three seconds, three minutes, three days, three weeks, or three months... but as surely as there is rain in a raincloud, which is happily gathering more and more moisture and heaviness, there is an indubitable certainty that it will eventually rain, and rain hard it will, on the practitioner's parade of ecstacy.

And as the (inexperienced) mystical seeker suddenly snaps out, or slowly comes out, of his more than probably selfish, unconsciously immature, and likely vestigial, 'bliss-out'... his consciousness will more than likely, come down hard upon the stony sidewalk, of ordinary reality.

But, there are always more than a few seekers, who will remain ever deluded.

C. C. C. 125-2

Never having had such a blissful experience, nor even a tiny glimpse, nor seen a single vision past the ordinary self; nor the profound mind ever having been properly prepared, nor trained, to grapple with the stratified glories arising out of empirical emptiness, then it is a near foregone conclusion, that certain consciousness circuits would be blown.

On the more than probable account of the seeker not having had any prior real spiritual realizations, and because of an overwhelming wham-bhang whopper of a mystical experience happening seemingly just like that, right away the mind sets about to thinking something like the following... or if the mind is frozen, then the feeling body being *blissed-out*, imagines something similar to the following: "This is it! I'm Illumined! I'm Realized! The Light was so bright! Manjushri Himself appeared to me! Vajrapani is some sight to behold with the thumpin' of His holy boogie boots, and with all that sacred dust a 'flying about' me!".

C. C. C. 125-3

"And now that I am *realized*, I must go back to the people like the Buddha did and out of compassion teach the unenlightened."

And so the blind-bikkhu, paltry pandit, little lama, unmandated teacher, fully groundless wayshower, and bonehead boddhisattva... as humbly great and positively selfless he thinks himself to be... is falsely born in a fool's paradise of inner illusion and delusion... on a destined mission to save all sensitive and sentient beings, with all of the idiot compassion he can muster up.

No one on the Dharma Path it is said, can by merely adding upon his spiritual experiences of light and insight, (his) yidam appearances and deity visions, (his) shamatha practices and samadhi states, etc., (and in totaling these up), say that: "Now, I have (in my possession), the BUDDHADHARMA MIND".

C. C. C. 125-4

Part II

The Buddhadharma Mind is not a mind that can be claimed by the percipient mind, or any mystical experience.

Ten thousand such percipiences and supernatural experiences, whether they be blissfully sweet, ecstatically-seizing, or thunderingly full of fulgar and intuitional flash... and (let us) throw in those clear-eyed states which are transcendentally tranquil... none of these, can squarely, or remotely, even in their totalled-up experiential aggregate, compare *quid pro quo*, to even one of the Enlightened Buddha's *tathagata thoughts*.

The Ten Mix-Ups of Non-Identical Twins and Their Ensuing Embarrassments

C. C. C. 125-5

Perhaps, if a disciple, through the progressive stages of practice on the path, arrives at that experiential state called "space-like emptiness", which tends to blow the wind out of the sails of the self, or of the notion of an apparent 'I' claiming to be real... and if, through further work of gaining greater insight and salient wisdom through even more practice, the disciple reaches the shores of what is termed "illusion-like emptiness"... which sees through the veils of all phenomena conditionally arising... and if, in the stabilization of both types of 'emptiness awarenesses', he consciously combines the two as being co-dependent and coetaneously arising with the now directly-awared 'true Emptiness', (or what is termed, 'the Ultimate Void of Non-Being')... then and only then, with whatever deeper Insight and transcendental Wisdom gained and with the spontaneously-arising, effortlessly filling, and consciously seizing of the very empty mind by the Buddhabodhi-Chitta Enlightened Mind, one could perhaps say that at that moment, Buddhahood paid a visit, and blessed the you that once and nevermore, will exist (as it was).

C. C. C. 125-6

However, for the sake of being more realistic, this sort of ultimate, Superior Realization is usually a roaring river's discipline, and an ocean's infinite surging, of constant practice away.

On the other hand, all continuous, spiritual work and practice, helps one get nearer to the shore of *becoming*... or of incarnating that transcendental, emanatory aspect of the Buddha, which, for want of better terminology, is simply referred to as Auric Fragrance, or Golden Radiance.

C. C. C. 125-7

Part III

An experience is an experience is an experience.

Experiences are ten rupees a dozen on the spiritual circuit... which today, operates somewhat like a "Buddha and Barnum's Circus of Meditation".

A meditation ebbs and flows; an experience comes and goes — you go into it and get deep into it; yet, you always come out of it.

However, a meditation, or a spiritual experience, well-integrated, is usually accompanied by a particular insight, or relative realization.

On the other hand, genuine Enlightenment, authentic Awakening, or true Realization, has little or naught to do with any kind of experience, exceptional understandings, intuitive contemplative insights, or arriving at sudden, relative realizations, (or eye openers).

Divinely authenticated Enlightenment, with its accompanying ground of continuous Bliss undergirding the all of experience, whether it be mundane or spiritual, involves a Direct Knowing, or Clear Awaring of everything and nothing at all, which spontaneously and naturally compels the consciousness into a total merging, or complete Identification with the Basic Inherency of Absolute Emptiness... coalescing unitively and arising simultaneously, with the ground of an Infinite Expansion, or Illimitable Fullness.

C. C. C. 125-8

Once *realized*, Realization remains.

It is There-Here, interpenetrating guilessly through all dimensions and time constructs.

It is There-Here, inherently so, awaringly so, and it is stable, and simple, and humble, and continual, and oh yes, it is *Here* and *There*, for REAL.

Indeed, it is going to take an infinity of spiritual experiences and an infinitude of hands-on material experiencing, for anyone to grow to even a measure of the BUDDHA's Enlightened Ankle.

BUDDHAMIND is not itself an experience, nor is it the totality of all experiences lived.

It is, rather, a total emptying of the consciousness of self, and of self experience.

It is synchronously, a total clarity of Self-Identification with the VOID, which innately fills all space, inner and outer, if inner and outer, really Are.

C.C.C. 125-9

Part IV

Enlightenment is an integral Radiant Awakening which in practice, becomes the primordial ground of one's own Unborn Being, in the universe.

Ever thereafter, in conjunction with the expanded understanding and true realization of his Bodhisattva Vow, the sadhaka or disciple, being ever forgetful of self, strives ceaselessly for the conscious awaring of his radiant Awakening, in contact with all sentient beings and things in the world.

Real experiencing and experiencing the REAL is an inherent *sine qua non* which comes meaningfully at the apogee of the Dharma Path.

Spiritual experiences are often blissful and rewarding for that part (of us) which is (merely) human. Once again, however, it must be stressed that they do not, in their totality, 'add up' to Real Enlightenment.

True Realization is the Dharma Path well integrated within and without, and humbly shines as a radiant mote of golden dust on the great Tathagata's Toe.

C. C. C. 126
(Commentary in four parts)

Part I

The cover of a book may fool a fool. The face and outer appearance, and the clothing of a man can do the same. The eyes however, if you know what to look for penetratingly, almost never lie — unless someone is a truly superb actor.

However, even then, you cannot keep untruth out of the eyes for too long — because both the inner light and the cast of the gaze, especially while that person is not looking, will unwittingly betray the proficient pretender, or accomplished hypocrite.

A pure heart always shows up in the eyes; true wisdom, even more so.

Sweet calmness and inner absorption are reflected in the subtle glow and gentle cast of the face. The blessings of a Buddha come to the fore in the grace of spontaneous gesture, honest directness, simple efficiency and gentleness of movement.

C. C. C. 126-2

To the knowing eye a hypocrite is spotted immediately; and to the clairvoyant eye of absolute mind clarity, such a false one is seen coming even before he takes a step forward. The bands of truth around the body and those of golden wisdom around the mind, (the head), are absolute in their tales of verity and revelation.

The golden nuggets of a fool's wisdom and the real thing, can very easily be mixed-up as being of equal worth and value, by the untrained eye, (or mind).

The true man or the pure disciple, is what he is through and through, and the slightest fault or tiny imperfection, which may unconsciously tilt the balance between Knowledge and Wisdom, is thereupon, directly tackled, uprooted and compassionately brought out to the light of his close inspection, and then slain, in order that it rise no more.

The false man, the tepid disciple, or the hypocrite lama, however, lets a multitude of such 'little imperfections' and 'insignificant weaknesses' go by, and before he knows it, he is knee deep in a swamp of slippery leeches, sucking away slurpily at the light of his being.

C. C. C. 126-3

In the dedicated disciple's important quest to win the right to wear the hood of true Bodhisattva-ship, there is no room for small flaws, faults and defects to go by unattended; where, if done so, to the critical point of cultivated contrapositivity, there is apt to be a major loss of accumulated merit... and where, if escalated to a major critical point, the cape of activated compassion could actually be rent, and the bodhisattva vow itself could bow forcefully broken, before the unattended burden of faulted neglect.

An imperfect lama of hollow heart hallows not nearly enough, the holy hood of (the) precious Buddha Mind of Bodhisattva-ship.

C. C. C. 126-4

Part II

There are the hypocritical lama pandits, lay and ordained, who prostrate before the BUDDHA, and do all of that which is anticipated of them and is of right regulation, but they perform all of it mainly for the sake of the form — that is, all for their looking good in front of a visible, (or invisible), audience.

These sort of lowly lamas, or deceitful disciples, devote not themselves to helping all sentient beings and creatures, but rather to maximizing the (hidden) ambitions of their shrewish selves.

Such polluted pandits will facilely prostitute sacred authority.

They will apathetically throw away all pure aptitudes, (that ought to be carefully cultivated); and may ensorcel to themselves certain psychic powers, in order to impress people and gain influence, or promote popularity.

They may even (partly) believe, or (smoothly) convince themselves that these powers are holy, but in the main, it is in manifest truth, (bottom line be said), mainly a 'see what "I" can do attitude', and please take note of my 'psychic' powers and 'spiritual' prowess.

C. C. C. 126-5

It is a recognized truism that everyone feels that he is (innerly) somewhat greater and potentially more, than what the present presently presents, as a projected picture of the self. No one knows it better than the false lama, pretender, pandit, or heavenly hypocrite.

But of course, out of laziness, insouciance, heedlessness, impatience, or what not, such a one would rather pretend to be an advanced, initiated, or realized being, than actually work hard and dig deep, to exact that which is of the Highest Order within him.

The moral, modest, simple and devout, whether layman or ordained, is also aware of the supreme perfections and pure heights to be attained; and, of course, knows that everyone has the inherent potential within their being to do so... but the tendency in too many of these common folks is that they are not educated, are never pure enough, can never try or do enough, to ever reach the heights of buddhahood, or enlightenment — it is all so far off, so (friggin') far off, and seemingly 'beyond the beyond', for their impure, ignorant and unmeritful selves to attain.

The Ten Mix-Ups of Non-Identical Twins and Their Ensuing Embarrassments

C. C. C. 126-6

Part III

The upright man is one who has a pure intent and proper motive. The impure man is one who has a double intent and dubitable motive.

It can be stated that once the Dharma Path is entered upon, and the feet of the disciple are solidly oriented to heeding the Call to (eventual) enlightenment, then all of the heart's attachment to (the things of) the world, are left behind in the dust of his Divinely-polarized departure.

Henceforth, there is no compromise vis-à-vis the compassionate ideal of serving beneficently the cause of all sentient beings and creatures.

'Head and heart' do now singly bow to the Buddha's (very Empty) Mind.

It is conversely cognized, however, that the knowledgeable hypocrite is commonly caught compromising his ethics, morals and principles, for the self-oriented, (therefore selfish), exigencies of the moment. Deplorably, his loosely-sworn oath and halfhearted bodhisattva commitment, are directed (obliquely) toward the service of self. Sadly, his word becomes slippery as slime and his dharma path turns as deadly deceptive as quicksand. His mind grows divided, his heart untrue.

C. C. C. 126-7

Part IV

The impeccable lama always has a right purpose which is irrefutably impersonal.

The false lama nearly always has a dubious purpose which is indubitably personal.

The true lama's essence of mind is always inherently pure in his caring for others, and is always oriented toward a detached, but compassionate service towards all.

The deceitful lama's mind is always caught in a double bind and a double kind of (subtle) service to self, whilst pretending it is for other, and his presence of purpose is nearly always, conditionally compromised.

Please do not be deceived by any tinsel antithesis to Authentic Enlightenment.

A hypocrite's inclination is to artfully and cunningly use the impact and influence of the law of impression in order to sway, influence, or mesmerize everyone, right into his personal breadbasket of false excellence and pretended merit.

C. C. C. 126-8

His antics can be likened to the obvious, or sometimes subtle, struttings of a pandit peacock, who, in self-deceptive sincerity, conceited vanity, and displaced (egocentric) pride, blindly honors and bows to the naga of a charming, narcissistic self... a smug, big mind.

An open-hearted, non-realized lama opts for the gratification of a highly delightful intelligent self, utilizing the positively magnetic means of a colorful, highly hypnotic personality. Moreover, he cryptically gives an active voice to an apparently unitive, collective effort in the modern philosophical field, known as 'evolutionary consciousness', (there is such a process), or an 'evolutionary enlightenment', (no such animal). Also included, is the manipulative stratagem of a popularly delineated, intelligentsia researched, smartly applied, integrative-inclusive-synthesizing sense of sociology, history and culture, and a comprehensively-integral-visionary psychology, psychotherapy, and spirituality.

However, the fact of the matter is that, once Enlightened, always Enlightened... (*if* Enlightened).

The Being, or rather the consciousness, evolves with the evolving Truth as it is NOW known, and expands horizontally 'ad infinitum' and very little, vertically.

C. C. C. 126-9

Evolutionary known knowledge, or relative Truth, metamorphoses naturally into the state of the completely Unknown and ultimately, into the dimension of the virtually Inconceivable Unknowable.

The true man of real Knowledge gives his whole heart to the Lord Buddha and from the awakening fount of his blossoming Buddha-Heart, he alone cares for the nondual reality of 'enlightened compassionate Wisdom', which he forthrightly gives away to all.

The true man of real Knowledge knows that though he has nothing, he continues to Hum in his inner (hearse) self, the modern (old) mantra of: "Don't worry be happy!"* and humbly knows, (being in the *patience* 'paramita' mode), that eventually, the abundance of all things (of significance), will one day, be added unto him... upon some obscure Tathagata moment of Now.

With an utmost purity of heart and with a mind bent upon his Bodhisattva Vow, he goes simply forward and lays down the natural way of the Dharma Path devotedly, and this for all of the Buddha's younger disciples, who are in the buddhafields of daily contention.

* A song composed by Bobby McFerrin, but the original saying is literally from a speech given by Sathya Sai Baba of Puttaparti, Andhra Pradesh, India.

The Ten Mix-Ups of Non-Identical Twins and Their Ensuing Embarrassments

C. C. C. 127
(Commentary in twelve parts)

Part I

The next theme considers the Mad-Hatter Lama, or the Budh* Berserker Lama, versus the ordinary lama, who has gone (just) plainly berserk.

The former is whole-heartedly, crazy-solid on the Dharma Path, wherever it may happen to be and in whatever form, (or non-form), it may take.

The latter, however, has gone right off the path's deep end, and has laid down his spirit's sanity, and everybody else's fair chance, at equanimity.

A Budh Berserker© Lama boldly bazooka's away all that may block Enlightenment, as well as knocking the bottom out of the bemoaning bleaters on the Path.

---

*Budh or Buddh, being the root syllable for Bodhi, meaning 'awake'; therefore, by implication, the 'Awakened One', and thus, refers to the Buddha. In this book of commentaries and for literary utility only, the use of 'Budh' instead of 'Buddh' has been chosen by the author.

The terms "Budh Beserker", "Budh Berserker Lama", and "Budh Berserker Siddha" are under copyright© 2011 Orange Palm Publications. All rights reserved.

C. C. C. 127-2

Such an exceptional Bold One will bazooka the path itself, and blow it to smithereens, if he sees that it is impeding a certain clarity of understanding; or is encouraging some form of false security, crystallization, or still-growth in consciousness, upon the intrinsically, non-descript Dharma Way.

Now, the ordinary mind and the ordinary man go hand in hand.

The ordinary mind is concrete and crystallized; the ordinary man is common and conventional. The ordinary mind's thought continuum is self-bound and security-based; the ordinary man's occupation consists of whatever is normal living, alongside the customary upkeep of the status quo.

The Spiritual, but non-fanatical, Budh Berserker shakes you up, to the very core of whichever-whatever self is false. He makes the very bones of your existence rattle like so many wooden chimes in the strong wind of His Presence.

The very flesh of the self is stretched and extended beyond the bounds of its careful folds. And the sorry piece of earth on which the flesh seems secured, shakes under the mantric thump of his Buddha sandals.

The Ten Mix-Ups of Non-Identical Twins and Their Ensuing Embarrassments

C. C. C. 127-3

The whole known body and mind universe quakes in uncertainty, and shakes in the fear of losing its common wits, and customary hold upon familiar reality.

The Budh Berserker pounds and pounces upon your pound of flesh, and he assaults your fenced-in acre of intellectual territory. He relentlessly raids your hard-worked cognitive cornfields, just as a cute reminder that none of it is yours… and he lets you know that the time has come for you to let go of your stuffy hold on all illusionary possession, like 'me-and-mine', and 'me and my' stuff.

The Budh Berserker is blatant, straight up, and lionhearted in his boldness to awaken with a spine-chilling roar, all those who are caught sleeping in tombs of comfort. There is an urgency in his voice; there is heat in his mantric drone; there is a compassionate angst in his fierce cry to liberate the sleepy 'I'. There is an earnest caring for *'les endormis de l'existence'*.

The Budh Berserker is authentic in his antics; his (slick) capers are not for show, but for effect. Spontaneously inspired and divinely motivated, he calls for all sentient beings to WAKE-UP! WAKE-UP! WAKE-UP! WAKE UP!!

C. C. C. 127-4

He cares not for the studied manners and self-conscious mannerisms of the gesturing body; nor for the selective bend and particular biases of the mind. He percipiently knows that behind the genteel and gentlemanly hypocrisy of any unenlightened mind, there is the gross, grasping 'I' who always looks out for No. 1.

The more greedily the 'ego' grabs, the more the 'I' wants the whole cream pie. The more the 'false personality' insists on the defense of its stuff and turf, the more the mind of man struggles in quiet desperation, and the more his spirit suffers a separative polarization.

No matter what his struggle and no matter what his suffering, man must be taught, (often the hard way), not to identify with the suchness of pain, or even with the cessation of such... for pain is pain, and it is nobody's cancer but pain's own basal identity, being what it is, and expressing itself as it does, in suffering *this* or *that*, disquieting condition.

And so it is, in reference to all antipodal states of feeling, sensation, and emotion, whether it be pleasure or pain, happiness or unhappiness, peacefulness or conflict, restfulness or agitation; patience or impatience, inclusiveness or exclusiveness, self-composure or anger, contentment or envy, lovingness or jealousy.

C. C. C. 127-5

None of these polar opposites belong to anyone. They just cannot be identified with for long. They cannot be owned, since they come and go like the wind. They are merely expressing what they were, energetically and basically, created to express... that is, objectively qualifying any subjective appropriation, or collective allusive expropriation.

It seems apparent that whilst on earth, pain, suffering and unhappiness co-arise simultaneously, spontaneously and equally, with states of pleasure, well-beingness and happiness... and that the whole shebang is karmically and Self-choosingly calibrated.

Hell is only heaven inverted. Evil is the word 'live' spelled backwards. Therefore, evil is that which involutes, or retards evolution; and thuswise, halts the upliftment of consciousness towards heaven, or a state of en-light-ened living.

If it is true that all opposites are co-existent and co-dependent arising, then, in reality, "All's well with the world", even if things, circumstances, or events, apparently aren't.

In other words: "Even in deep shit, *reality* peacefully sits and tranquilly perdures".

C. C. C. 127-6

Part II

The whole wide world seems to go *wham, bang, wham* upon the 'I' am... in order to help man realize that the whole wide world is the inescapable 'who-done-it' of the *I-you me-we* of all human existence.

In other words, the whole wide world arises as the *I-you we-us*, being guilty of all creative doings, positive and negative — and men and women, folks and everybody, that is the nature of the whole wide, innocent world, and really, nothing and nobody, is to blame... yet, the *I-you-me-we, all-as-one* are responsible for the creation of this, or that specific situation, contentious circumstance, or worldly condition.

Whatever comes up in life, do not smother it. "Let it arise naturally", says the Budh Berserker, "for absolutely everything, positive or negative, has an essential Budh nature. Do not go crazy and blast it out of existence, just because you do not like what seems to be objectively arising, along with you".

The Ten Mix-Ups of Non-Identical Twins and Their Ensuing Embarrassments

C. C. C. 127-7

"Be patient, because you never know, (and yet, you do monadically know), that absolutely everything which comes up in life does so specifically for you to someway accept and somehow bless... and to say gratefully "thank you, thank you, Lord... for every single thing has a (kindly) karmic aim, and is there for your gentle release, my evolving babe".

The personal consideration of everything in life is consciously undersigned by the official stamp of your subjective acceptance, or rejection, of anything... so that every single interpretation of intent, meaning of motive, significance of thought, affect or effect of emotion, purpose of speech, and consequence of action... is entirely of your own choice, and creative making.

Do not, therefore, irresponsibly accuse someone, or point an incriminating finger of blame at anyone... or towards an event, situation, or circumstance, in overly critical overtones... for is it not evident that the other three finger barrels, are aimed at you?

Rather, be alert, be mindful, and take immediate responsibility for your selective section of samsaric suffering; and stand tall and distinctively challenged, by your own being's call to Liberation.

C. C. C. 127-8

The Absolute is absolutely in everything.

The Ultimate is ultimately in no-thing.

It is up to you to radically intuit that the latter pronouncement is innately empty of any substantial meaning in anything that seems real.

The former saying, on the other hand, is utterly devoid of any substratal meaning in everything that is real.

C. C. C. 127-9

Part III

The Budh Berserker is one who gets drunk on yummy yogurt and on all things physical... alcoholic beverages being only another substance equal to, (and of no less, no more importance), than any other stuff... it's all yummy.

The Budh Berserker is one whose mind gets naturally high on everything and nothing... and just Being is bliss, (and hell), and that's the Blessing, (and curse), of It All... no more, no less.

Total acceptance of Life with a joyful openness, and facing the face of multivariegated Reality as It Is, along with the many diverse countenances of constantly arising phenomena, are but the abc's, (or elementary stuff), of eventual Liberation.

Because the Budh Berserker is free, he can in all liberty choose to go left, or right; do this, or that; to engage himself in a negatively polarized situation, or a positive one, (usually too easy).

But he does so, ever without repression, nor suppression.

C. C. C. 127-10

He is not mind-bound, nor desire-bent, to act in terms of the world's purblind predilections; nor according to man's morally biased nature of musts and must nots; nor even, to what seems culturally apropos, or not; nor ethically, to what one should do, or not do.

He cannot be infected, nor affected, by the world's (self-inflicted) toxicities; nor coaxed, (against his will), to enter any of humanity's limitative incarnational incarcerations, or private prisons of self-punishment... all on account of an abstract sense of shame, or an ideational sensation of sin.

The world pretends to be sober, yet, in actual existential fact, the world is blind drunk on the 'I'-labeled booze of desirable duality; and because of the ensuing fogginess of vision that ineluctably follows, it consistently fails to see both reality as it is, and Reality, as Is.

C.C.C. 127-11

It is somewhat like an alcoholic who ardently denies that he has a problem with alcohol, and overconfidently thinks himself capable of both clarity of thought and cloudless visibility.

Alcohol, when taken in excess, is the cause of a delayed reaction time and a distracting sleepiness, and of many other debilitating symptoms that go along with the depression of the central nervous system; but the alcoholic, especially when bleary-eyed drunk and near black-out, will excessively insist and be personally convinced, (and he may even sound convincing), that all is under control and that he's got a solid handle on things... somewhat like the false desire-bound 'ego' which blindly claims to be in complete control, (that is, to say, clearly in charge), and therefore, master of the host consciousness, as well as the captain of his (sinking) ship.

C. C. C. 127-12

Part IV

Nobody in society is more doggone sober and dynamically awake than the Budh Berserker.

In fact, he almost has to go mildly berserkers, or at least make a good show of it, using startling shock tactics and other discomfiting what-nots, just to get today's over-blaséd people to lift a slightly raised eyebrow, or lend a half attentive ear to what he is saying, or doing... just in case there could be a wild ace in the average crowd of existential snorers, who may surprisingly possess the potential capacity to Awaken.

However, almost all of the sleepy people sleeping on the sleepy shores of phenomenal samsara, judge the Madhatter Berserker to be some sort of a rude dude... a mad someone, without any of the social graces, who is crassly indelicate, noisy, insulting, strident and definitely deranged; a brazen, crazy, rock-the-boater, whose stormy, (sometimes uproarious), mock and shock manners, are just plainly, in-your-face, outrageously annoying.

The Ten Mix-Ups of Non-Identical Twins and Their Ensuing Embarrassments

C. C. C. 127-13

One of the Berserker's recurrent messages, which he tries to really drive home, because it (almost) always goes into one ear and comes right out the other, is that "there is absolutely nothing stable, nor secure about the phenomenal world... never has been, just ain't, and never will be".

Right here in this uni-verse, there is at best, a relatively major, somewhat mysterious, somehow incomprehensible, sometimes conspicuous, seemingly chaotic, orderliness.

Take for example, the celestial charts of galaxies, constellations, nebulae, black holes, the phenomena of stars, the various suns, moons, and planets; or, take the very basic example, of just the simple seasons... so much variety and sometimes so much predictable unpredictableness, yet always freshly mysterious, miraculous, and even awesome... are they all in their dependable regularity and eternal recurrency, and in their subtly dynamic, studied paths of disciplined movement and interminable change.

C. C. C. 127-14

Constant movement, constant change — a most wonderful, rhythmic and cyclic discipline, to integrate and ride — since it is always with us, right-in-our-face every single day, and we find it in every minute of every hour, which passes relentlessly by.

We all know intuitively that no second will ever wait for any of us to catch up with it, because it is inexorably on the move, tic-tocking, micro-tumbling forward, and is instantly, (irretrievably) gone.

And yet, here we are silly-clinging to the past, in both a memory generating manner and a feeling experiential sense.

We grasp at what goes by in beauty and pleasure, and cloy to the gratifying present, (or push it away, if unpleasant)... in order that things and events provide us with a secure comfort base of sameness, conventional similarity and commonplace status quo, (with a certain hypothetical assurance of unchangeableness)... which of course, equips us with a false sense of sheltered safeness from change and an ego-inoculated crystallization of consciousness. It is not only anti-nature... it just cannot be done. And yet, everybody tries.

The Ten Mix-Ups of Non-Identical Twins and Their Ensuing Embarrassments

C. C. C. 127-15

Are we that slow, insecure, stupid, or what!?

Or is it that incomparable 'escamoteur', the great horrific illusionist, the pronounced personality prestidigitator, the almighty 'ego'... which is practicing its magical phantasmagoric fantasy number on us... and is pulling the wool over our eyes, again and again and again, in a seemingly continuous 'tour de force' of phenomenal bewitchment.

A sunrise is no surprise, and yet, we are full of bliss and rejoicing at its glorious rising.

A sunset is no surprise, and yet, we are full of rapture and awe at its ecstatic setting.

The four seasons are no surprise, and yet, we await each one with a subtle (pleasurable) impatience, and we enjoy their coming, and take delight in their special delivery.

We find in Nature a mindful, disciplined (slow) movement of constant subtle change, which nourishes the human being with a living happiness that is basic to the health of his own planetary, earthy physical being.

C. C. C. 127-16

Any prolonged passivity, or sustained (static) form of inaction, however, brings on a pained physical condition, and a contracted consciousness of ego-suffering, on account of the transgression, (or neglect), of the fundamental law of movement and change. It takes the energy of (both gross and subtle) movement to generate any sort of transformative expansion, and this law applies even to the domain of spirit evolving within the matrix of matter.

It is so, also, with a set of muscles that are either too long at rest, or in too long a state of protracted contraction: these conditions will invite, along with the production of various acids, the accumulation of anaerobic toxins to produce the obvious effect of a lack of tonus, or oppositely, that of severe cramping... with the resultant relevance, (often excruciating), of pain... and all this because of a basic disregard for the simple (natural) law of essential movement.

Because Life is constantly on the move, the all of life, (personal and impersonal), must perforce, also move, and not stand still for long. Man must accept this 'movement' conditional clause, as being fundamental to the metamorphing of his overall well-being.

C. C. C. 127-17

Intermittent movement and alternate change as primary laws of nature, must be recognized, respected, anticipated, and obeyed.

Yet, by some odd inverted thinking and quirk of lopsided reasoning, man seems to fear the compelling aspect of (necessary) cyclical change, which must mandatorily accompany all things that are conditionally relative... which also applies to all of that, which is naturally relational.

It is more than obvious that stretched-out staticism leads to still-growth, and that undue passiveness, or inhibiting paralysis of any kind, is debilitating, detrimental, isolationistic and often destructive to any progressive state of affairs — whether it be the world's economy, its sciences, religions, philosophies or art movements — and particularly, when applied to an entire culture, civilization, or the whole planetary body itself.

C. C. C. 127-18

Things just cannot stay the same.

It is a basic fact of living and a critical condition of Life.

It is a Primary Law of the organic structure of Existence Itself.

To go counter to, or even, to ignore the above Law of Change, is to invite the descent of involution, or still-growth, upon the consciousness, which in turn, negatively conditions the mind and paves the way to an *existential* stroke of the spirit.

In addition, it brings down upon the human heart the thunderbolt clap of fear and mistrust, which signals a closing of the doors of enlightened compassion, and activates the curse of the apparent death of evolution, within the human psyche.

C. C. C. 127-19

Part V

Though admittedly and legitimately necessary for certain target objectives and purposes, rules and regulations remain in the main, a fixity of relativity... that is to say, a 'fixation of consciousness' within a narrow band, or fixed frequency, of mind.

For instance, eating regularly three meals a day at specific times is both a mental and physical fixity, that is to say, a fixed habit based on a hypnotic credo. Sleeping eight or 'x' amount of hours every night, is a fixity. An addiction to the game of seduction, and all obvious overindulgence in sexual expression, are really dependency issues, or expectative sensual fixities. Sexual abstinence itself can also, (and often does become) a "fixed fixity"... a sort of shame-based, or guilt inverted, anti-natural, contra-pleasure, purist fixation.

There is often found in individuals a can't do this, can't do that, 'limitative' fixity.

In fact, all that is concrete, customary and conventional, in whatever area of endeavor, can easily, (often unconsciously), become a restrictive and counteractive, hypnotic fixity.

C. C. C. 127-20

And so it is with beliefs, ethics and morality; as well as all (man-made) laws and ways of doing things... even unto those 'fixed' personal habits of hygiene, dressing, and engaging oneself in *puja*.

The Budh Berserker is nearly always an ardent enlightened eccentric. He loves to knock down all retardative images, and can't help but smash to smithereens all those fixities of consciousness that induce man, (more or less), to complacently sleep his whole life away. His favorite dance is doing the "monster mash" all over the corpses of the fallen icons of the "living dead"... that is to say, of all those things, physical and non physical, that are adjudged to be of the realm of the 'unawakened mind'.

To the Budh Berserker, there is nothing holy, nor especially sacred, other than that of Self being spiritually moved in every act, thought and word, by the sacred empty Hallow-Hollowness of Existence Itself.

All else is the mere play and shallow apprehension of the world of appearances, made real in the reflective and refractive image of man, *'as if'* it were all *real*.

C. C. C. 127-21

Part VI

Real is Real and false is false. There is no trucking nor compromise, to be had with Reality. Either you got it, or you don't.

When the Real gets a hold of you, it's for real; you either have Realization, or you don't. You are either Enlightened, or you're not.

Flashes of illumination just won't do... especially if you are standing in front of an Enlightened being who has It... or rather, It, the Void, has him... in its non-differentiated, non-dual, non-hold.

A flashlight brought outside, and used in broad sunny daylight to find something, is a lunatic's gesture (of show).

No small light, nor false light, nor (any) crazed light, can get past a bone fide Berserker's great Lighthouse, or blazing Sun of Realization.

Your light is either Real, or not real.

All flashlights, (or false lights), brought out into the broad daylight of a Budh Berserker's steady illuminating Presence, is pure energumenic folly.

C. C. C. 127-22

No untrained, ordinary, conventional mind, whether it be of man or monk, woman or nun, can do naught but express its natural, innate monkey nature.

In calling a spade a spade, may we speak frankly, and plainly refer to the possibility of a monkey-mind monk, or to a monkish monkey-mind, without being necessarily irreverent.

Recitation of rosary, or mala, is by far and large for those, (and there are few exceptions), who have not as yet awakened to either the full Light of Realization, or to the All-Emptiness Mind of Supreme Awareness; and who have therefore, not attained, and even less stabilized, such high transcendental types of crowning consciousness consummations in the contemplative life, nor (obviously), in daily life.

If a disciple is still meditating on one of the seventeen (to twenty) progressive 'empties', then he has not as yet entered the Great EMPTY, (or the Absolute VOID)... into which all of the empties empty themselves as mere tributaries, rivers and streams, into that great Universal Ocean of All-Consuming, (even of Itself), COMPASSION.

C.C.C. 127-23

That Limitless Ocean of Compassionate EMPTINESS remains essentially not only undivided, undetected, unplumbed, and 'Unknown' to the ordinary consciousness, but it goes without saying, that it remains inherently 'Unknowable', by all of the normal states and standards of lower mind.

A man of Realization is his own bright Source of Illimitable Light; and well-resourced is he in his own Radiant Luminosity.

Discipleship under a Berserker Illuminate, or a realized Budh Being, is about as safe and secure for the ego self, as stepping into a live mine field. You just don't know, you can't ever know.

In a Budh Illuminate's Omni-presence, a disciple must always be at 'acute attention', more than just being 'totally present', and he must be in the 'heightened senses' of the Self, as much as possible… for, just one inattentive 'faux pas', just one fractured second out of the present time frame, and Pow!!! — the ego self gets not only K.O.'d but smashed to near fatal psychological smithereens, and sometimes, (if the student is ripe), to near total egotistic annihilation.

C. C. C. 127-24

And if the disciple, (out of egoic terror), dares try escape from the invisible safety net of a Budh Berserker's occult intent... that is, away from His purportedly crazy, not crazed, Guru Krupa... then, possible neurotic cleavage and dual existential absurdness, may just lie in wait somewhere in the individual psyche's, 'Sleepy Hollow-ness'.

C.C.C. 127-25

Part VII

The Budh Berserker is tough to be with — so what, he didn't promise you a lovely lotus swamp.

Ego's gotta go and in Berserker lingo, you ain't got a chance in hell to get uplifted into a spaceship by some smiling E.T. of idiot compassion, and make good your escape.

A Budh Berserker's cosmic cyclopic eye has your I's little b-u-t-t in constant view. And that's the way things are... with B.B.

So there's no compromise, just tough compassion. There is no real sense of security, just complete unpredictability — and this on all three levels of the physical, mental-emotional, and spiritual.

Nonetheless, there is one sure thing and one thing alone that you can count on, (or be sure to find somewhere written in real invisible ink), within the Budh Berserker bible.

It concerns the unwritten promise, (or Bodhisattva Oath), which deals with his complete fatherly commitment and his entire motherly devotion, (although he will rarely admit to it), to his beloved disciple's true Awakening.

C. C. C. 127-26

The real Guru is a rigorous guru; the true Guru is a tough guru.

The strong Lama is a firm lama; the genuine Lama is a powerful lama.

The Budh Berserker, however, seems to be for sure, only one thing... a blissful, one-eyed, one-horned, two-fisted, exacting, absurd, trying, baffling, lustful, unfathomable, absolutely divine, son-of-a-b_ _ _ _ and a boisterous b_ _ _ _ _ to boot.

That just about sums Him up pretty good.

Consequently, because of the Budh Berserker's fiercely rebellious nature and rowdy, (often raw), independent character, disciple subservience is mostly not welcome as a behavioral characteristic in his unorthodox, rather radical training of students.

B.B. outpictures his anti-classification type of deprogramming program as an open, wild, unpredictable, non-sequential, always arising, and definitely progressive endeavor toward real Attainment, or what some call, the Serious Work of Liberation.

The Ten Mix-Ups of Non-Identical Twins and Their Ensuing Embarrassments

C. C. C. 127-27

Part VIII

If disciple subservience is not welcome, then an alert, open surrender, ever mindful to the moment, is.

What is really demanded by the Budh Berserker is an acute sense of self-responsibility, and a hefty, healthy sort of self-reliance, that can actually be counted upon, even in the midst of a complete self-surrender, no less.

C. C. C. 127-28

If the disciple is in heavy difficulty and needs bailing out, then only at the exact moment just prior to his drowning, or at that very precise psychological, critical despairing point, when and where, it seems the disciple just cannot take it anymore, not even for one second longer... well, after that second has passed, and maybe after another second has gone by, and oops, another is somehow slipping by... then only, with a rushing blur way beyond the slow speed of light, the Budh Berserker will careen around the corner with the burning incense smoke of screeching indian rubber and with one swift, sure movement rescue his disciple with all the tenderness, love and care of a boxing mother-kangaroo... or with the authoritative, detached, (but secretly loving), rally of a doting father for his beloved son, or daughter disciple, more precious to him than the sun and moon in a somewhat dubitable, impersonal sky.

The Berserker Lama is one who has gone irrevocably beyond sanity, or insanity.

He fears not insanity because he is the rare one who has already, adventuresomely, lost his mind. His condition is gamely helpless and high-spiritedly, without hope; it is a zillion light-years Beyond, being repaired.

The Ten Mix-Ups of Non-Identical Twins and Their Ensuing Embarrassments

C. C. C. 127-29

He is one who is delightfully irretrievable, deliriously irreclaimable, and completely undone. He is way past mending. He is but a glad ragpile of Light and underneath it all, he cannot be found. All human reason, (and reasoning), has gone-gone-and-gaily-gone beyond the Beyond; he is already, eons ago, irredeemably ruined.

The B.B. Lama has already gone existentially kaput... (before birth).

With the insightful arrow of his clear light awareness, he has penetrated the (bull's eye) of the Great Empty; he has pervaded the Absolute Void and disappeared into the consummate Naught-ness of black boundless bliss.

The Omnipresent Wisdom and All-Knowingness of everything, which is an inherent quality of the Naught-ness of Pure Emptiness, re-awakens to the extreme n^{th} degree of sensitivity, the sacred vow which the Budh Berserker Bodhisattva took for the sake of all sentient beings, a thousand million million years ago.

C. C. C. 127-30

And it is with a renewed sense of infinite Vigor that his Divine Anguish of Compassionate Caring for all of the little children of the Lord Buddha's delusory domain... is once again rekindled, as a huge inextinguishable flame of forever Loving Compassion, in his Burning Heart.

C.C.C. 127-31

Part IX

Somewhere, in the Limitless Immensity of Inner Space, there cryptically beats a Budh Berserker's non-circumferential Heart of Fiery Existence.

The very Immeasurableness of the Illimitable Infinity of the Inner Universe, pointedly hints at the great, hidden measureless depths of Eternal Knowledge, which is available to such an Accomplished One, as a 'BUDH BERSERKER' Buddha.

Why men and women of ordinary mind usually insist on their staking, cornering and personally planting a corny acre of farmland, (material happiness), right smack in the middle of what is the great existential flow and flux of the forever-moving, forward-and-onward universe, is beyond the Berserker Guru's kindly ken of trying to comprehend, what to him, is pure unadulterated folly and outright self-deception.

C. C. C. 127-32

The aforegoing deceptive, descriptive, declamatory dilemma is to the Budh Berserker Lama, but a bunch of utterly wasteful, wholesale, (delusional) bunk. It bespeaks of men and women whose unthinking minds have gone, (to put it mildly), truly bonkers... but do not know it as yet... or, for one reason or another, are unwilling to pause and see the insanity of it all.

On the other hand, there are truckloads of modern gurus, especially in the occidental countries... although the east still has their countless jeepfuls, and their packed 'nine nuts' to-a-motorized-rickshaw full of them... who have boldly, but blindly, taken on the role of 'berserker' guruship... but who are in the main just plainly bonkers, or simply, simon-pure schizoid.

Notwithstanding, this new slew of pseudo gurus, whether they be occidental, middle eastern, or far-eastern, (oriental)... as well as an alarmingly growing number of black-market gurus and lamas... are about as annoying to Authentic Spirituality, as the collective consciousness of about twenty-two thousand two hundred hard-nosed fleas are, on a water buffalo's back.

The Ten Mix-Ups of Non-Identical Twins and Their Ensuing Embarrassments

C. C. C. 127-33

These purblind and (oft) prurient gurus and lamas, do like to latch on to their little, or big piece, of land and hermitage; their sacred cave, holy cell, (and cell phone); deer skin or tiger skin, meditation mats, or contemplation quilts; and their usually many holy this, holy that, estimable titles; their 1 to 108 worldwide ashrams, and umpteen roomfuls of rare thankas and valuable Buddha statues, and dear Dharma icons, in their myriad array of monastery complexes; and they have the bad habit of dependently hanging onto, or being metaphorically hung, by their 100 to 108,000 rather disturbed, but seemingly devoted disciples.

C. C. C. 127-34

Part X

The prevenient little water buffalo gurus who think they are raging bulls of spiritual insight, on account of their very deluded 'mastered' selves, must somehow be swished back to sanity by the bushy tail of re-integrated right thought and correct incisive discernment. This is usually done by means of a rude awakening of direct and discriminating 'shock treatment', orchestrated by a capable B.B.

An example of such a hard-healing treatment might mean the bold use of such skillful means as the awesome thunderclap 'Roar of Reality', whose roaring sound instantly cuts clean through all spiritual foolishness and falsity; and annihilates all fallacious, fraudulent and feigned claims, or plangent acclaims, to professed superior states of Bodhisattva-ship, even to those of exalted Buddhahood.

C. C. C. 127-35

Another hallowed example of the use of an exalted modality utilized by the Budh Berserker for the radical healing of pseudo-guru delusory greatness, (whether the so-called guru's comportment be overly flamboyant, or is bent factitiously-humble in self-avowal), is by the radical means of the searing descent of the great "Vajra Illuminator Bolt", which instantaneously clears the air of any trace of untruth and brings in the Real Truth, mercilessly compelling It to bear somberly upon all states and conditions of human hypocrisy... such as alleged allegations of grandiloquent benevolence, Ossianic saviorship, pompous pronunciamentos, and spiritually 'shy' Wonder Woman, or spiritual Superman proclamations.

Let it bong forth abundantly clear, that it is only a humbly realized, (ordinarily meek, modest and kind) 'Daddy Cool, Budh Berserker for-the-Buddha', who can responsibly utilize, (rarely), the likes of such mature and radical siddhis, and only with the Purest of Intent, which is reserved for the purpose of either the (vital) healing of the spirit, or the uncovering of Real Truth, as It Is.

C. C. C. 127-36

Consequently, rare are the times that these radical, (clearing house), siddhis are to be used.

Also, to be distinctly noted, is that ordinary, bonker-gurus are just not worth even a fraction of the expended energy needed, for such an Awakened Buddha's "Lion's Roaring".

The Ten Mix-Ups of Non-Identical Twins and Their Ensuing Embarrassments

C.C.C. 127-37

Part XI

A veritable Vajra Berserker Lama strikes like a battalion of armed thunder, scattering to a panicked roar and rout, the discordant sounds of the world's army of lies.

And His hot Lightning Breath brings forth a fiery clarity, cutting clean through the clouds and vapors of humanity's deluded vision and diluted version, of things 'as they are'.

His Flaming Light razes to the ground the dark forests of ignorance that make men and women ache and suffer.

And new grasses of Wisdom sprout up; and new trees of Truth grow.

And extraordinary new roots of Knowledge take hold and fair flowers of renascent Beauty spring up in the newborn Buddhafields, of a B.B.'s compassionate Presence, under the watchful gaze of his starry Spiritual Sight.

C. C. C. 127-38

The Budh Berserker's high task of crazy purposeful Will is, of course, primarily to awaken man to the pointed realization that in order to save himself, he has got to quickly figure out, (and intuitively grasp in this very moment), that his beautiful house of consciousness is hopelessly engulfed in flames... and, of course, the Mad Lama set it on fire in the first place!

The average man's house of beliefs is on fire presently and he's got to get out right now! Out of his silly, straight-jacket life of security... with its safety ploys, guarantees and maintenance of the status quo... and this without delay, if he ever chooses to live a life of 'greater abundance'.

The new neurotic narcissism, or egocentric, constrictive 'repli-sur-soi', with the ensuing 'mal être' which often plagues the modern materialistic mind, is extremely constraining and exhausting, to the Inner Spirit and its inherent sense of Freedom.

It is time to get out of your stuffy, smoking, burning house, Now! The lion's roar of your individual Spirit calls for Total Liberation, nothing less, Now!

The Mad Lama, (for his part), in being a true blue BUDH BERSERKER, just has gotta do, what he was born-Realized to do... PHAT, PHAT, PHAT!

The Ten Mix-Ups of Non-Identical Twins and Their Ensuing Embarrassments

C.C.C. 127-39

Part XII

Beware and be aware! When the Mad Lama gets mad, and hot sparks of True Enlightenment go flying about, in the ten known directions of the universe from his open, orange palm, or from one of his mighty, flaming, pointing fingers; or from his all-consuming, wisdom-filled, fiery gaze; or from the molten core of his quixotic, impartially impassioned Personhood, whose very Essence Presence, of course, is fully identical with, and equal to, the Buddha's own Radiant Effulgence... and from that moment on, everything and everyone directly or indirectly in contact with Him, is bound to be on the hot stove of the BUDDHA TATHAGATA's evolving consciousness for all sentient beings and diversified creatures, anonymously cooking away!

The weak lama, whose middling mind has gone off the deep end of delusional madhatter guruship and who is wontedly whacko, is a very distinct critter compared to the real Budh Berserker Lama, although sometimes, he is superficially similar in eccentric antics, and unconventional behavior.

C. C. C. 127-40

The B.B. Lama has plumbed the Absolute Void and become solidly Empty; the former has fallen through a hole in his head and become quite emptied of his senses.

The major differentiating factor is the fact that in the falsely illuminate lama, true depth of discrimination, real power and pure wisdom, are grievously lacking.

As a closing polemic, the following issue is the crucial controversial point, where we separate the men from the boys, in the (Tibetan) lamaism of Real Realization.

The weak lama's mind which has gone off the deep end, has done so principally because of his incapacity to take in the full penetrative point of the vajra arrow of Blazing Buddhahood, deep into his own heart, where soundly-hilted, (as it ought to be), should go to the very inbeing, of the sacred syllable of 'Hung'.

Crucially, the delusional madhatter lama comes up terribly short, for he has definitely not, in true Bodhisattva fashion, learned to die irredeemably, upon the sacred arrow shaft of self-avowed selfless service to all sentient beings and living creatures.

C.C.C. 128

To the ordinary mind, a Siddha Budh Berserker, is a strange sight and a strange-seeing being.

Siddha Budh Berserkers are not at all, 'regular' spiritual stuff; they are, from the very first glimpse of them by the common man, a totally fresh surprise, conveying to the consciousness an unexpected, completely unorthodox aspect of expressed Realization.

And express themselves they most surely do — on anything, against everything, or for nothing at all... even when utterly quiet.

They can make a show, or a no show, of all thought and mental notions, even though they hold to no thought, no notion, nor opinion.

In a sense, authentic mystical manifestations and veracious phenomenal appearances and occult hints, cues, indications, suggestions and even (astounding) demonstrations (of all sorts), these are their usual modus operandi of expressive communication.

C. C. C. 128-2

Even, if for them, all spiritual inference, intimation and innuendo, are all inexpressibly in vain, and that the all of it is fundamentally illusory, Lama Budh Berserkers will in practice, (and with lots of humor), still exemplify what (in modern parlance), we have come to call the natural 'rebellious state'. In their case, they can, therefore, (with tongue-in-cheek), be casually identified as 'mystics without a cause'.

They are the occult originals and why, indeed, should there be the need of a mysterious mystical cause, when all is mere Emptiness, (anyway)?

Supernally Divine Siddhas and Buddha Budh Berserkers are the ultimate occult purists. They are without any real religious form.

Their purpose is true purity, ('Pure Emptiness'), for purity's sake.

The Ten Mix-Ups of Non-Identical Twins and Their Ensuing Embarrassments

C. C. C. 128-3

Their Nondual Dharma schemata respires without the constraints of obligatory rules and regulations; of ordered study, sadhana and imposed disciplines; or endless other requisites and prerequisites, (all of them phony), for the mean minor attainment of an imagined, last-word progression of sorts... relating to the stages, levels, states, degrees and gradations of an eventual, so-called *enlightenment*, upon a programmed, well laid-out dharma path — as if the Dharma could be reduced to a few planned primer courses, for the expressed purpose of gradual Illumination.

Their teaching methodology is quite forthright; in fact, it is not a method at all, but rather, a hands-on approach, a direct transmission of the ineffable teachings... something like a raw leather sandal, or a frying pan, being bopped on the head as "whack, whack, whack, bam, bam, bam, you good-for-nothing, sleepy, idle, lazy hunk of honest ham — Wake up!".

"This is the way to do it. Simple, not complicated; it's like this — not like that, or that, or that!"

"But honestly, don't believe any Truth I may tell you, even if it is real."

C. C. C. 128-4

"Now listen to me, to what I am saying!", the Master would chastise a disciple and he would then, suddenly and promptly, cease to talk, and completely ignore the disciple. And if the disciple, in speech, thought or gesture indicated that he was in the least perplexed, or felt that he was being ignored, then again, the "whack, whack, whack, bam, bam, bam, you-no-good-ham" rigamarole, would be hammered into the disciple with a repeated warning, "I told you to listen to me, to what I am saying to you!". And again, before the disciple would have a chance to give voice to any frustration, or even form a decent question, or reasonable objection, the Master would quickly turn around, and promptly shut out all form(s) of normal communication — thereby leaving the disciple simply dumbfounded as to what to do, or even, how to soundly Be.

"The sky's the limit!", is not exactly the right slogan for them.

The sky is rather, a mere pillow to place your head upon, when you go into the dream-Awake mode at anytime, (no set time), during the day, or night.

C. C. C. 128-5

Siddha Budh Berserkers have no set routines; they mock most rituals as being barren and essentially empty.

They are known to be notorious practical philosophers of the type exemplified by "put your money where your mouth is, or be gone".

Being rather independent and original thinkers, they get instant divine diarrhea, on hearing the proud pandits spouting off their silly spiritual stuff, and mulling over mystical abstractions, and muttering utterances of mere metaphysical speculation.

And they casually and usually, urinate on holier-than-thou charlatans, whom they can facilely spot a cosmic mile and a half away.

Siddha Budh Berserkers are down-to-earth, practical, supra mystics, often grubby, gruffy, grumpy and gravelly-voiced. But they can also (humorously) demonstrate spiritual expertise at will, and be absolutely ethereal in the literary and musical fields of endeavor; and some do sideline-duty, playing the role of inspirational 'ghandarvas' to various superb singers and illumined poets.

C. C. C. 128-6

However, they are often crusty-looking and take on the humble and mean roles of carpet weaver, shopkeeper, masseur-masseuse, clerk, just a cop-on-the-beat, corn-picker, fisherman, town grocer, husky-trainer, Maitre D, overworked waitress, construction worker, and what else, a high-rise window washer.

And they tend to remain in the main, rather simple, and they guffaw like Goofy, full of joy and tender laughter, as they apperceive with natural delight and unconditional happiness, either the vicissitudes or pleasures that the ordinary world purely and daily offers, to their brain-senses, neurotransmitters and nerve synapse machine, which is, (supposedly and seriously), the body-mind construct.

Budh Berserkers consciously walk, run, dance, sing, meditate, do mantra and puja, eat, drink, play, have sex, do marathons (of all sorts), and cry out "Enjoy, enjoy, the Here is Now!"

But they do so, really resting and laughing uproariously, upon the conditional clause of "do not get caught, nor addicted, to the bliss or bafflement, of it all!"

The Ten Mix-Ups of Non-Identical Twins and Their Ensuing Embarrassments

C. C. C. 128-7

The 'this' or 'that' particular pleasure or pain, (of any moment), is but a passing ephemerality of sensation, (soft or intense), featuring the greatest technicolor show in three-dimensional, personal living, this side of the cosmos.

Budh Berserkers may often seem to be simple, naive and innocent of mind, but they are not; they may seem, on the other hand, to be complex, sophisticated, noble of thought and refined of manner, but they are not.

They know it is, rather, all part of the illusionary con game, which is the experimental and experiential, material world.

To the experienced and wise Budh Berserker, all is rapt emptiness and flawless absurdity.

Budh Berserkers may prefer, if they so choose, to be crude; they may take immense joy in being downright bawdy.

No doubt about it, Budh Berserkers are living symbols of an upended, impassioned breed of Guruship, or Lamahood.

C. C. C. 128-8

It stands to conservative reason that a true blue Budh Berserker, is oft a secret source of embarrassment to all of the three serious vehicles, of the traditional Buddhist establishment.

Publicly and clandestinely, most monastic monks energetically study and often sustain an ongoing, open admiration for the radical works and liberal lives of the (eighty-four) famous, almost superhuman Mahasiddhas, or the almost unknown, supermundane Budh Berserkers.

They set them up as being real spiritual heroes, but nowhere, (in the last few centuries, at least), has there been a veritable place for a Padmasambhava, a Tilopa, a Dombipa, or even a tiger-riding Sahara, in the stultified, (and stultifying), atmosphere and disciplined, staid airs of near yesteryear's, (or even today's), modern Buddhist monasteries of traditional academia, sadhana, and practice.

The magnificent Mahasiddhas or the sublime Budh Berserkers, of the past would find today's university monasteries to be ruefully, little more than stifling coffins for the eternally free spirit of Bodhicitta enlightenment; and probably, much to their chagrin, they would argue a good case also, for too many restrictions being placed upon what should be a more ecumenical demonstration of the Bodhisattva Vow.

C. C. C. 128-9

To a perfected Siddha Master, or to a true-blue Budh Berserker, every single earth encounter, (if it is unaware, or unconscious), simultaneously occults and erodes the topsoil of Truth.

Yet, this poor planet, is deemed by Them to be the very same experiential platform that serves as the precious wish-fulfilling jewel, of potential Enlightenment.

The earth planet is truly a precious Ornament of Liberation, a veritable golden opportunity of realizing the possibility of one's going from individual personhood to a state of all-inclusive Buddhahood. But in the very same breath, it is also adjudged to be a very empty material bauble of highly creative, but essentially unsubstantial, mindstuff.

And yet, whilst the individual is in earthly incarnation, it is considered an important truism to realize that 'my precious earth, is also, my precious teacher' — for without the opportunity of earth experience and earthly matters mattering, nothing veritably essential would ever dawn or flower, within the individual consciousness, that really makes a difference.

Even the Lord Buddha Himself touched his hand symbolically to earth, as being the primary witness to his authentic Enlightenment.

C. C. C. 128-10

Without the Earth opportunity and the Earth plane experience, the Buddha would not have had the chance to become what he became, because of what he was before he became what he had come to become, in order to demonstrate to the world, what he really was, before he came.

In other words, the mysterious universal plethora which is the outflowing panorama of planetary appearances, is at center, essentially Empty.

The whole wide world drama altogether, is but an ongoing passionate play, taking place in the present of what was once the Is, and now, (in appearance), is and is not.

Ah, so much for crystal (rational) clarity!

The earth is indeed a mind bauble whose centre is joyful Emptiness.

Few know that Emptiness Itself, sprang Lightfully from the crown of heaven, coupled to the bowels of earth… a bolt of lightning being the symbol (of its fiery transfer).

Therefore, praise Earth and praise Emptiness… for both are equal partners in the Great Play of Life.

C.C.C. 128-11

Budh Berserker Lamas prefer a philosophically spontaneous expression of self, (often quite lewd and ribald), combining together a bemused metaphysics and an earthy mysticism, which are at once, both awfully confusing and esoterically illuminating.

To them, such an eclectically bizarre approach is great fun, and is considered a fantastic exercise in pure oblique pellucidity.

Again, Budh Berserker Lamas can be lewd, luscious, lustful, and loving... sometimes, all of that, at once. They love sex and no sex, equally.

They are superb healers, miracle workers and great inspirers. The birds, domestic animals and wild creatures warm up to them; all sentient beings and living creatures seem positively magnetized by their all-encompassing presence.

Budh Berserker Lamas transform, change, or turn lives around, always for the universal and greater good.

C. C. C. 128-12

They may, or may not, (secretly) fly the spiritual skyways; levitation by itself, is too simple, just too boring. Women and children find themselves spellbound, enthralled, enraptured and captivated by them; and are often delightfully drawn to them.

Budh Berserker Lamas introduce a new twist into trite fidelity, and put a whole new interweave into the meaning of (being) deeply faithful.

They are non-attached, true-hearted human beings and are demonstrably devoted, utterly divine, buddhic bohemians.

Their breadth of vision is awesome; their world work is consciously counter to world orthodoxy.

Radically, do they stand against all religious gospel and caustic are they, (often in a light and humorous way), in condemning all spiritual tradition that is sectarian, conservative and conventional, or purist, isolationist, stiff in form, and strict in authority. This to them, is the main cause of all religious insipidness and spiritual unimaginativeness.

All staidness of spirit and stagnation of mind, must go.

The Ten Mix-Ups of Non-Identical Twins and Their Ensuing Embarrassments

C. C. C. 128-13

The Buddha Dharma should always remain a living, "create-the-path as-you-go" conditional clause of the Way Itself.

A particular predilection of a Budh Berserker's enlightened Awareness, manifests as a marked penchant toward the extirpation in all domains of life, of all dead deeds and withered leaves of the past, especially those that have no practical relevancy, to the times and exigencies, of today.

And this, of course, includes literal *(dead)* translations of past spiritual works, that have, (because of their uninspirited literalness and uninspired translation), no pertinent power, punch, or adaptability to today's ever expanding, evolutive mind.

Much of a Budh Berserker's medicinal abilities, or healing powers, are deliberately directed toward the care, healing and salvageability of societal sicknesses; and of all those social ills and inequitable injustices, which militate against the proper cultivation of a sane spirit, within a future benevolent and compassionate society.

C. C. C. 128-14

The breadth of vision of a Budh Berserker Lama is verily awesome.

His radically innovative writings, as well as his dynamic translations of past, renowned and scholarly works, are nearly always pragmatically noteworthy.

His words of wisdom are veritably profound pieces of script, cryptically fitting into an infinitely sizable jigsaw puzzle of ineffable Truth, sometimes offhandedly written on the inside layer of some cigarette foil paper; or, on plain, slightly rumpled, green-lined, yellow, legal paper, (folded in half); or, just for fun, on some of today's thinnest, popular, crane white or baby pink toilet paper.

Whatever country, city, part of town, hillside village, or luxurious valley, he may come from... one thing seems common to all Budh Berserker Lamas... and that is, factually and simply, the resplendent nondual nature of his Buddha Mind in the manifest mode of the incorruptible, Mahamudra Siddhi Seal.

Tough, difficult, irksome, almost impossible, it would be for a charlatan monk, or hypocrite lama, to ever copycat that Occulted Seal!

The Ten Mix-Ups of Non-Identical Twins and Their Ensuing Embarrassments

C. C. C. 129

A bone fide Bodhisattva will always bounce upon the scene at no better timing than when there is absolute need, indeed.

A bone fide Bodhisattva gives of his noble body boldly, bawdily, and absolutely, and is always Buddha-radiant and Buddha wise, according to sentient need, indeed.

A bone fide Bodhisattva gives of his noble mind, being the best of its kind, and puts his everything behind it to free all sentient beings from bondage, belief and bind, according to compassionate need, indeed.

A bone fide Bodhisattva gives of his noble speech in compassionate heat, in order to treat the seared seats of consciousness, of those innumerable selves sitting on the hot stove of samsaric griefs, and here, there is much liberating need, indeed.

A bone fide Bodhisattva gives his all, and gives again and again, and whatever gain that he gains, this gain he will give again, but never in vain... in exchange for the sentient (earthly) pain that the Buddha's blessed rain will help to wane.

C. C. C. 129-2

A bone fide Bodhisattva is he who is what he is, a Buddha-graduated Lama Lord, kind to the compassionate core of his Enlightened Being.

His Buddha's hood humbly covers his glowing head, and he stands bowed in the radiant recognition of a million thanks, for all the favorable times his tripartite personhood has had, to serve and uplift with the gift of inexhaustible vigor, the Maitreya Buddha's infinite number of precious little ones... until that great glorious future day, where all sentient beings can at last, be gathered and salvaged.

On the other hand and in another reality, an erring and false lama can pretend to accomplish a variety of impressive bodhisattva deeds, and being a good pretender, may attract a generously giving, but blind following of fawning fools.

Rest assured, however, that any such dishonest accumulation and dishonorable increase of the false mint of undeserved merit, (a spiritual fool's false gold), will in all probability, end up being held-up by some greedy and astute robbers of grace, on the way to the fat lama's bank of self-investment.

The Ten Mix-Ups of Non-Identical Twins and Their Ensuing Embarrassments

C. C. C. 129-3

So, let it forthright be stated and let all monks who sit in meditation, be unambiguously admonished, knowing that all involuting self-seeking activities and self-serving deeds, heedlessly harm, damage, upend and upbraid ignobly, the noble, princely and excellent Bodhisattva Vow.

Do not partake in such ignominy.

C. C. C. 130

The breath of a bone fide Bodhisattva benefits everybody, wherever on earth such a receptive body may be.

Out of the movement of mind, everything arises. Quieten the mind and nothing dares stir.

Discard the activity of mind and nothing can ever rise, for all potentially that kinetically Is, reposes quietly in Nature's Womb.

This primal Womb of Nature is known by Higher Mind as the Wisdom Mind of Emptiness... out of which the silent stirrings of thought is born.

When this sort of Wisdom Mind does stir, or move, it is cryptically referred to as an 'effortless effort', or 'actionless action'.

This, of course, apperceptively assumes that no minuscule amount, nor even one iota, of discernible karma is incurred in Consciousness, nor cosmically recorded.

C. C. C. 130-2

No discernible karma is being apparently incurred, or factually activated, basically because the self, (or the 'I' notion), is not being attracted, actuated, nor implicated, in the flow of whatever is forever *becoming* form, potential material activity, or possible circumstantial event, on the physical plane.

Manifestation, or physicality, seems to happen, because of the switching on of the basic, tripartite 'mind basket' of perception, apprehension, (via a focussed attention), and projection... being conveyed unto the screen of a being's 'self consciousness', becoming (paradoxically) objectified as the subjective 'I', acting out in a duality polarized, phenomena-dependent, phenomena-arising, universe... which, in its twisted contrapositional turn, only seems to become 'objectified' to the eye of the 'subjective I'... but is, in both fact and relative reality, almost entirely personalized, and person actualized.

C. C. C. 130-3

Now, being acutely aware of the essential emptiness of the constantly projected show of gross and subtle physicality, which transpires without, as a moving time stream, or a flowing river, or movement of the mind-matter continuum, within a 'self'-consciousness of 'I'; and this 'I' notion, in its falsely identifying itself event by event, with the whole outflow of the phenomenal process of Manifestation, outrageously submits the SELF's inherently 'Original Nature' to deliberately suffer the impact of an 'initial objective motion', followed by the shock of an 'Initiatory movement', right into physical samsara.

The Awakened Bodhisattva, however, consciously awares forth a singular sense of detachment and succeeds to maintain a strong sobriety of non-attachment vis-à-vis the phenomenal dynamics of Life's Manifestation, and life's existential dilemmas. Whatever transpires, whatever happens, he doesn't seriously break a sweat.

A thought, an action, a bird peep, or poop, every single thing, rings the bell of Mindfulness in him, and he never forgets the Divine Being, or Non-being, that he Is.

C. C. C. 130-4

"Come what may, if you keep the self-seeking self, out of the way, you keep the negative at bay, and the river of life flows on its merry way", he just might say.

The Exalted Bodhisattva does not deliberately stir, nor muddy the depths of life's karmic pond. He rises, rather, out of the depths of samsara's pain upon the purity of his heart's white lotus, and walks lightly upon the waters of life. His upraised palm showers beneficent blessings upon every head and his serene Buddha smile reassures those who are having a hard time.

'Skillful means', being a living Bodhisattva's working tool, refers to his masterful circumstantial use of Bodhicitta, the enlightened, heart-rooted compassion. In other words, it is activated golden wisdom working with impartial love, co-dynamically, in all the divergent fields of human endeavor, through Not-him.

The true Bodhisattva is a pure, blameless buoy of bottomless blessings blissfully buoying up the world's condition of blind, benighted boredom. His lovely nature is as soft as yummy butter in a pan of stainless steel cooking up a luscious meal for someone's spirit, under the heat of life's tests and trials.

C. C. C. 130-5

The lofty Bodhisattva is gentle, light, calm, and truly genial. He is a Balm of Bliss and ever slight-of-self in all Dharma disposition; and yet, he is adept, adroit, deft, resourceful, and a real ace at addressing the samsaric, karmic conundrum of suffering to be found almost universally amongst all sentient beings and creatures.

His noble mind, being made up solely of the sterling substance of Emptiness, cannot ever deceive, nor even conceive of being double.

He cannot delude, defraud, or dupe anyone in any sort of material fraud, or samsaric duplicity. Some lesser lama might, perhaps, because he is still retaining a semblance of the separative, grasping self. However, in His being a true blue Bodhisattva through and through, the genuine Buddha article, cannot.

The union of a heart-rooted compassion with that of the Wisdom-mind within a genuine Bodhisattva, gives spontaneous rise to the sacred Circle of Emptiness around and about Him, within which all who live, may thrive as a protected child of the Dharma. His bone fide Bodhisattva Vow, vows to use all of the skillful means at hand to successfully accomplish his Task, for the ultimate peace attaining benefit of all suffering sentient beings.

C.C.C. 130-6

The Light of pure selflessness in him, at work in the specifics of any circumstance, condition, or situation, is easy to spot... for it glows with the gold of the Bodhisattva's tender concern regarding the discriminative, multifaceted use of the most precious of Tathagata Tools, known popularly as the *'skillful means'* of a true Peaceful Liberator, or Knight of the Empty Light.

From the aforementioned description of what an authentic Bodhisattva is, in his Non-separative Identification-with-other, whatever his suffering... the false one, (out of a sense of shame), need not be described.

These then, are Simhananda's contemporary, contemplative commentaries regarding **"The Ten Mix-Ups of Non-Identical Twins and Their Ensuing Embarrassments"**.

Glossary

Adi Buddha: Primal Buddha.

Arhat(s): 'The Worthy One'; a direct disciple of Buddha, a high initiate.

Atisha: (980/90-1055) Buddhist scholar who systematized the method for generating the enlightened Mind (bodhicitta). Founder of the Kadampa school of Tibetan Buddhism.

Bikkhu: A fully ordained male Buddhist monastic; lit. 'beggar' or 'one who lives by alms'.

Bodhicitta: 'Awakened mind' or 'mind of enlightenment'; 'citta' signifies mind and heart, and 'bodhi' awake or enlightened; it entails the vow to attain enlightenment for the benefit of all beings; therefore, the Great Compassion.

Bodhisattva: A realized Buddha who has made a vow of service to all sentient beings, sacrificing his own immediate and complete liberation to compassionately aid and uplift mankind.

Budh: 'To awaken', 'to know', or 'to become aware'.

Candrakirti: (AD 600-650), a renowned Madhyamaka philosopher, from the Prasangika school of Buddhist logic; he wrote the famous commentary the *Prasannapada* ("The Clear Worded") on the Buddhist sage Nagarjuna.

Dharma: 'Divine duty', daily right action, the way of Truth, the cosmic law of Spirit; the 'great norm' underlying the manifested, or phenomenal world; finally, the inevitable law of underlying karmically-determined rebirth.

Dharmadhatu: A notion of the True Nature which permeates and encompasses phenomenal existence; the existential space of absolute reality.

Dhyana (ic): Meditation or contemplation; the state of deep stillness and inner poise reached in advanced stages of meditation.

Dombipa: 'The Tiger Rider'; king of Magadha; he was initiated by the Guru Virupa into the mandala of the Buddha-deity Hevajra. He was a saintly man who practised tantra secretly for twelve years before he abdicated in favour of a contemplative life in the wilderness.

Dzogchen: Lit. 'great perfection'. It is called 'great' because there is nothing more sublime; it is called 'perfection' because no further means are necessary. According to the experience of *dzogchen* practitioners, purity of mind is always present and needs only to be recognized. Brought to Tibet by Padmasambhava and Vimilamitra, 8th Century.

Ghandarvas: Celestial performer, musician. Male nature spirits; part animal, usually a bird or horse. Messengers between the gods and humans.

Kadampa: A school of Tibetan Buddhism founded by Atisha in the 11th century emphasizing the lo-jong (training of the mind), the bodhisattva ideal and monastic training and discipline.

Kleshas: The five primal causes (obstacles) of suffering as described in Patanjali's Yoga Sutras; 1) avidya (ignorance); 2) asmita (egoism); 3) raga (attachment); 4) dvesha (aversion/replusion); 5) abhinivesha (fear of loss or fear of death).

Kundalini shakti: Occult energy stored primarily at the base of the spine; its controlled, upward awakening (by the Consciousness) along the spine to the head's crown chakra, (Brahmarandhra), is one of the main goals of numerous spiritual traditions.

Mahamudra: Direct practice for realizing one's Buddha nature; one of the highest teachings of the Vajrayana school of Buddhism, as revealed by Tilopa; through this meditative system, the practitioner generates the realization of emptiness, freedom from samsara and the inseparability of the two.

Mahasiddha(s): Lit. 'Realized One' or 'Great Adept'; in the Vajrayana tradition, name given to the eighty-four great Indian adepts, or eccentric ascetics who mastered the teachings of the Vajrayana Tantras.

Maitreya Buddha: The future World Teacher. He will inspire humanity to see itself as one family, and create a civilization based on sharing, economic and social justice, and global cooperation.

Manjushri: Bodhisattva of Great Wisdom; in Tibetan Buddhism Manjushri embodies the incisive wisdom that dispels the darkness of ignorance.

Marpa: (1012-1097) Renowned yogi of Tibet, also called Marpa the Translator; through his travels to India, he brought back to Tibet many teachings, including the Mahamudras and the Naro Chodrung (Six Doctrines of Naropa); root guru of the Kagyupa lineage.

Maya: Illusion; relative phantom-existence; the created universe as being a play of illusion, and giving rise to false knowledge, untruth, and ignorance; the Veil which hides the Vision (of Truth).

Milarepa: (1025-1135) Famous Tibetan master and poet; founder of the Kagyupa school of Buddhism; one of his principal disciples was Gampopa who was also known as one of the two 'successor sons' of Milerapa.

Nagarjuna: (2nd century) Indian mahasiddha and prominent author of many Buddhist philosophical treatises; father of the Madhyamika (Middle Way) school; one of the Masters of the "Six Ornaments".

Naropa: (1016-1100) Well known Indian pandit and mahasiddha; disciple of Tilopa; he was an important figure in the transmission of the teachings of the Mahamudras; author of the Naro Chodrung.

Pandit: A Brahman scholar; used as a title of respect for a learned man in India.

Padmasambhava: 'The lotus-born' or 'the precious Guru'; a contemporary of the King Trisong Detsen, one of the founders of Tibetan Buddhism (8th Century) where he is venerated as the second Buddha; also considered to be the Protector of Tibet.

Paramita: 'Excellence or perfection'; 'to cross over to the other shore'. Associated with Mahayana teachings about the practices of the Bodhisattva (the Six Principles of Enlightened Living).

Puja: Ritual worship in which a deity is invoked in the form of an idol, or picture, and is propitiated as a Divine guest with offerings of flowers, fruits and other eatables, along with the recitation of appropriate mantras and an expression of relevant signs.

Rendawa (Shyönnu Lodrö): (1349-1412); a great Sakya scholar. Tsongkhapa's main beloved teacher.

Rinpoche: 'Greatly precious'; a title given to a highly respectable dharma teacher; a spiritual Master in Tibetan Buddhism.

Sadhana: Spiritual discipline and meditational practice; the duties and discipline of discipleship.

Sadhaka: Spiritual aspirant/student; a disciple; a chela.

Samsara: The wheel of rebirth, the process of worldly life; the cycle of rebirths that a being goes through within the various modes of existence until final liberation is attained.

Shamatha: Dwelling in tranquility; calm abiding; the meditative practice of calming the mind.

Siddhis: Psychic powers of tantric practice.

Sukhavati: 'The Blissful'; name given to the pure land, or western paradise of Buddha Amitabha.

Tantra(s): 'Treatise'; a set of scriptures in which esoteric teachings and occult practices are given; systems of meditation described in the root texts of Vajrayana Buddhism.

Tathagata: 'The thus gone one'; one of the ten titles of the Buddha, a term he used about himself as an individual who has brought an end to suffering and has reached nibbana (third noble truth).

Tilopa: (988-1069) One of the great mahasiddhas of India, the guru of Naropa; disciple of Nagarjuna.

Tsongkhapa: (1357-1419) The incomparable Buddhist scholar known as Je Rinpoche, who helped create the great Gelugpa school of thought in the late 14th century in Tibet; a glorious emanation of Buddha Manjushri; the monasteries of Drepung, Sera, and Ganden were founded through his inspiration, influence and activities.

Tushita: One of the six deva-worlds of the Kamadhatu, located between the Yama heaven and the Nirmanarati heaven. In Mahayana Buddhist thought, it's where all Bodhisattvas destined to reach full enlightenment in their next life dwell for a time.

Vajra: Lit. 'Thunderbolt' (cuts through ignorance), and 'Diamond' (destroys, but is itself indestructible). In the center is a sphere which represents sunyata the primordial nature of the universe, the underlying unity of all things. Emerging from the sphere are two eight petaled lotus flowers, one represents the phenomenal world (samsara), the other represents the noumenal world (Nirvana).

Vajrapani: A member, along with Avalokiteshvara and Manjushri, of the trinity of Bodhisattvas known as the Three Family Protectors. Vajrapani (Holder of the Thunderbolt) represents the energy of the enlightened mind, and energy that breaks through delusion. He dances wildly within a halo of flames, which represent the transformative power of Awakening.

Yidam: The term employed for a disciple's chosen personal deity used in meditation; a subjective spiritual guide, or divine protector.

Zazen: Zen meditation; lit. 'seated mind'; the practice of awareness, of bringing your attention, or concentration, to the present moment.